You Don't Speak Welsh!

Because of Dafydd Iwan
– whose music inspired me to learn Cymraeg

You Don't Speak Welsh!

SANDI THOMAS

ISBN: 086243 585 4

Cover photograph: Robert Jones

Dinas is an imprint of Y Lolfa

Published and printed in Wales
by Y Lolfa Cyf., Talybont, Ceredigion, SY24 5AP
e-mail ylolfa@ylolfa.com
website www.ylolfa.com
tel (01970) 832 304
fax 832 782
isdn 832 813

Introduction

For those in Wales it is sometimes a matter of necessity to learn Welsh but for others it is a slowly blossoming personal need. Oddly enough this need strikes even those of us who do not live in Wales, but are of Welsh heritage in another country. There is a strangely charismatic mystery about being Welsh, and it has nothing to do with country. It has everything to do with heart and soul and the intangible awareness of what is a part of you. For me, this awareness was gradual and grew upon me in proportion to the number of times I visited Wales.

With each new visit the need for the language became more intense. I began to know that there would come a day when I would learn Welsh. That day was always somewhere in the future, but my awareness of the fight for the survival of the language was always there. It was something that fascinated and drew me to the language, the concept that one's language would mean so much that one would go to prison for it. The idea that whole factions of people have devoted their lives to fighting to keep their language spoke to something in my soul. I began to realize that it was a last desperate gamble to save a culture, and therefore not just about language at all. Rather about an entire People, and that nation of People was what I, too, was descended from.

This fascination with the fight for the Welsh language ultimately led me to the music of the 60s, 70s and 80s in Wales, especially that of Dafydd Iwan and other nationalists. It was all in Welsh, that mysterious sounding language I was going to learn SOMEDAY. But I needed to know those words, I needed to understand what had been said and was still being said about being Welsh, about the language and the need to speak it. Suddenly that need became my need in a very immediate sense. It was the key to things I couldn't understand, and I wanted that key!

I began to teach myself Welsh and it was a terrible struggle. I bought Welsh dictionaries, which had to be specially ordered from overseas. I found a Welsh-language lexicon over the internet which helped me translate words. I began to arduously learn words and slowly understand snippets of thought in the songs I was translating. During this process something began to happen. I began to love the language, to want to hear it, to want to be able to say those words I was learning in a way that would sound Welsh! My need for information became a purely personal need to have the language and I knew that SOMEDAY was now here. I was going to learn to speak Welsh.

I lived in America. I knew I would have no one to speak Welsh with. I wasn't happy to settle for a brief, watered down American version of a Welsh class, offered only at two or three places in the entire country. I looked to Wales, and discovered something amazing and wonderful. Welsh was taught all over Wales! Schools taught it, universities taught it, private language schools taught it, night school classes abounded and private Welsh tutors did too. But I didn't have the luxury of time to do full semesters or year-long night classes. Sadly, I didn't live in Wales. And so I opted for a unique programme known as an Wlpan class, a month-long course of intensive Welsh. Six hours a day, five and a half days a week, I would take Welsh at Prifysgol Cymru in Aberystwyth for the entire month of August. I would learn Welsh!

It was only when I began Wlpan Awst that I realized what a task I had set for myself. It was then that I realized that learning Welsh is probably a lifelong occupation. It was also when I realized how much more than learning a language learning Welsh really is. It is about becoming something other than I have ever been. Something more, something better, something unexplainable to those outside the experience. I realized that the experience of learning Welsh must be shared; that there are many learners involved in the daily struggle, and the comradeship of learning is the ship that keeps you afloat. So, I offer this daily account of the struggle to all those who are actively engaged in the process of learning *yr hen iaith*. But I also offer it to all those who have dreamed that one day, SOMEDAY, they will learn Welsh, in the hope that it may make that SOMEDAY begin to happen now.

Dydd Un: What Am I Thinking Anyway?

Our first week's tutor is Rhys – with a doctorate in Welsh and a mischievous grin. He is also very short, which I guess makes him very Welsh! There are fifteen in our class – British, American, Canadian and Australian. Only four are from Wales. Strange thing, isn't it? One of the British women is married to a Welshman who doesn't speak Welsh. He also doesn't intend to learn. She needs it for her job in a Welsh office, but he says it's "too much effort". I've seen that attitude often in Wales. A friend in *Caerdydd* told me, "They want you to learn Welsh so bad, they ought to pay YOU to take it!"

At first everyone is very quiet, looking each other over. There are always the few assertive, authoritative types – but mostly just a bunch of strangers feeling a little intimidated by a room-full of strangers ready to confront head-on a strange and unfamiliar language. Yet there is also an air of low-voltage excitement thrumming through the atmosphere of the room as the instructor speaks his first words to us.

"Shoo my." He smiles at us.

We all look fatuously back at him.

"Sut mae?" gets scribbled across the board. Rhys smiles gently and says *"Sut mae?"* He gestures for us to say the same.

"Shoo my!" comes shyly from fifteen throats.

"Eto!" he says.

We stare blankly at him.

"Eto. Again… " he smiles.

"Sut mae!"

HELLO!

It had begun.

Around the room fifteen times we answer the question "What's your name?" *"Beth yw'ch enw chi?"* Looking at faces struggling to concentrate we answer, *"Sandi dw i", "Nigel dw i", "Mair dw i", "Telor dw i".* Each tongue sliding off *dw i* with confidence after the first try.

Already it is time for coffee and we traipse to the coffee room to sit at tables in awkward stiffness, venturing small conversations with strangers. Then back to the classroom and we learn to ask where everyone lives. *Byw*. To live.

"*Ble dych chi'n byw?*" (blay duck een bee-oo). Fifteen times – until we have all repeated it aloud. Then we are up around the room. A Welsh "cocktail party" of conversation. "Where do you live?" "*Dw i'n byw yn California*", or wherever else someone lives. We stumble onward, tongues wrapping around the unfamiliar phrase "Do een bee-oo," smiling in embarrassment or apology.

By five o'clock, when we are handed our first printed sheet of vocabulary (*geirfa*) and homework (*gwaith cartre*) there is a frantic feeling of being already overwhelmed by the rapidity of it all. My head is swimming with the phrases I've been asking and repeating all afternoon.

After dinner, when I confront my homework sheet and the list of first-day words and phrases, I stare at it bleakly. Where is this going to get me in life anyway? What is your name? Where do you live? Where are you from originally?

It's like kindergarten for adults in a starkly foreign, cumbersome and HOPELESSLY abysmal language three quarters dead and of no use whatsoever in America – in California! Or, for that matter, in Wales itself where everyone speaks English anyway and consequently CAN understand everyone else if they choose to do so. Stubborn, independent, nationalistic Welsh speakers clinging to an archaic language no one else knows, understands, or can even pronounce! It's all a grand mistake! I'll never be able to do it, remember it, CONVERSE in it!

Around me in town, at Safeway, on the Prom, I have heard Welsh being spoken – lilting and speeding words in a cadence impossible to catch up with. There is no way I will ever do that. What am I thinking of anyway? Welsh speakers will condescendingly pity my pathetic attempts at speech and move on to English to avoid the tedium of speaking with a learner.

I can't talk about it either, not with my non-Welsh-speaking friends who look at me as if I were an oddly deformed alien. They pass it off politely or hurry on to safer subjects. Or they bristle and posture and spit out words of condemnation. "Language Society troublemakers", "obsessed Plaids", "manic nats", "You know how they are up north…" How did I end up here? What romantic, idealistic pipe-dreaming is this? How can the siren song of long-ago-lost Welsh relatives be so strong?

I drop into bed at midnight with *"Dych chi'n byw yn Llanelli?"* running through my head. Where is Llanelli anyway? *"Gwela i chi 'fory,"* I whisper aloud for the sound of it on my tongue. "See you tomorrow." The next thing I knew, it was.

Dydd Dau: The Language Conundrum

Bore da! Seven a.m. comes too early. Latent jet-lag, new surroundings, too-hard bed and too-lumpy pillow have made sleeping difficult. I awake to "*os gwelwch chi'n dda*" running through my mind – spilling out in repeated whisperings. "Please." Rain, bouncing in pellets off sidewalks, the parking lot looking slick and wet from my window. An umbrella kind of a day.

I trudge down the hill, umbrella over my head, and through the empty buildings – a ghostly temple of knowledge. Then I hear Welsh rippling across a hallway, bubbling through a door. The advanced students. I look at them like a first-year law student looks at the District Attorney – the first-year med student at the neurosurgeon. Attainability about as possible as winning the national lottery. The lilting cadence follows me down the unlit hall.

I sit down in a new spot today, by new people. I smile. They smile. We share our frustrations and sense of being overwhelmed. A tenuous bond begins to form, shaped by our common desire and sense of ludicrous expectations for ourselves in the face of terrible odds.

Rhys, in lime-green shirt and dark-blue pants, sleeves a little too long for arms a little too short, eyes friendly behind wire-rimmed glasses, looks at us and says "*Sut dych chi?*" "How are you?"

We smile furtively, our secret fears having been shared with others, and the laughter bubbles out again. We are nervous, frustrated, apprehensive, and we are ready. We're off again!

Another round of "cocktail party" begins. "*Dych chi'n gweithio?*" Do you work? "*Ydw.*" I do. "*Fel beth?*" As what? "*Myfyriwr*", "*Athrawes*", a student, a teacher, around the room until a list as long as a page is formed, full of scratched out and scrawled letters equalling strange and scrabbly words.

We sit again and around the room we introduce ourselves and tell what each of us does: tripping up, struggling, repeating again, the strange words beginning to make some sense. The sounds no longer seem so strange. The *r*'s begin to break loose and attempt to roll, the *ch*'s that stuck like hard *k*'s in the throat yesterday are finding a little bit of depth and reaching for a bit of "wetness", which is the only way I can think to describe the sound of a Welsh *ch*.

I spent last night despairing of *r* and *ch*, pondering how Rhys could roll over his *r*'s and thicken his *ch*'s in just that right way that sounds Welsh. How did one do that? Am I trying too high in my throat? Is his a deeper sound? He says "more phlegm" – disgusting, but exactly what it IS when you think about it. It doesn't sound disgusting when a Welsh speaker does it. Then it is fluid, charming, exotic, and well – CELTIC sounding. Maybe I was born tongue-challenged! It won't bend, it won't flap, it won't vibrate. It won't roll into that wonderful "rrrrrrr" that accompanies Welsh *r*'s. Poor clod of a tongue! Poor throat that won't find any moisture to dredge up a decent *ch*! Hopeless language, so full of booby traps that shout "beginner", "learner", "amateur".

Amser coffi – coffee time! Then back for more – more lists, more conversation. "*Dyma Telor*" (here is Telor). "*Mae e'n byw yn Aberystwyth*" (he lives in Aberystwyth). ON we go. Just when I start to understand, to really KNOW what it is Rhys has asked and manage to find the right response out of all the words now filling my head, it gets more complicated. Like a runner jumping his first hurdle I leap over – and fall flat on TREIGLADAU.

MUTATIONS. Language here was hard enough without the newly sprung announcement that the Welsh language MUTATES. How sinister it sounds! MUTANT. MUTATING. MUTATIONS. Like a mad scientist concocting monsters from normal cells, the Welsh language concocts mutations of words, corruptions of letters. Try *Caerfyrddin*. Just try saying that. *F*'s are V's in sound. *Dd*'s are Th's. And, as if that wasn't enough, it now sprouts uglies – it MUTATES! It grows – becomes incomprehensibly deformed as *Nghaerfyrddin*. The tongue rebels completely. *Talybont* suddenly sprouts an "Nh" and becomes a weird-looking place called *Nhalybont*. These changes are startling enough, but they also have names that sound like an ear-and-throat doctor's list of symptoms. Nasal mutation. Aspirant mutation. They decidedly DON'T sound like things you would do to words.

My head is swimming with rules. After *yn*, after *fy*, when a vowel follows *yr*, when a consonant follows *y*. There is a scream building inside that wants to shout "No more!", and miraculously Rhys announces "*amser cinio*".

Lunch break stretches ahead and two o'clock seems vastly distant. But I can't get it out of my head. With every bite of sandwich words keep rhythm as I chew. *Gweithio, ond, pentre, dref.* They sift and collect and fly back up again only to drift back down as *ysbyty, cyngor, ysgol, ar hyn o bryd* – at the moment. AT THE MOMENT I AM DROWNING IN WELSH WORDS!

Take *llyfrgell* for a moment. What kind of a word is THAT? What horrific challenges for the human tongue can equal my attempts to say "*llyfrgell*". There must be an easier word for "library" than "thluhvuhrgethl". *Llyfrau* (thluhvrye), *llythyr* (thluhthur), *llwybr* (thloowebur) books, letter, path. The *ll* is the greatest challenge of all the Welsh-language challenges. I have been spitting and blowing my attempts at the sound all day but it never sounds like the *ll* that Rhys blithely pronounces.

Two o'clock arrives faster than I realize and it begins all over again. More monsters, hairy-eyed *Treiglads*, this time with the name of *Meddals*. Mutants from some other planet where words grow as long as tree trunks. Now I must remember that after "i" and "o" "p's" become "b's", "t's" become "d's", "d's" become "dd's", and "g" disappears completely never to be found again. Poor "g" – something like my own mind at the end of this day!

Cappuccino at three-thirty and everyone now sits together talking, smiling, letting loose. We're now Angie from Australia who's an artist, and Nigel from Basingstoke who's a teacher, and Mair from Paris whose parents are Welsh speakers who refused to teach the language to their children. No longer strangers to each other, we share our obsessions and compulsive needs to learn Welsh. We ponder the strange lure of this magical, horrible, wonderful and thrilling language. We shake our heads at our insanity, at the eccentricity of it all. Yet we are secretly proud. We are DOING it. We are attempting the impossible, facing down the jeers, the stares, the condescension. We refuse to give up our ridiculous, pathetic, beautiful, near hopeless dream of speaking Welsh. *Pam lai* (why not) reach for a dream? Somehow it is the quality of that *gwlad fach*, that little country of Wales itself, that has lured us on into the tangled web of Welsh.

"The biggest problem," says Rhys, "is that no one will speak it with you."

This, then, is the fate of beginners – sunk in the doldrums of "learner ostracization".

"If your pronunciation is off, they'll pat you on the head, say 'Oh you're learning Welsh, good for you', and immediately break off into English to continue the conversation." Rhys shakes his head. "It happens again and again."

Is it intolerance of learners? Is it impatience, not wanting to be bothered? Is it elitism? Language snobbery? Is it the Welsh not wanting to accept anything below their standards? Certainly it can't be threatening.

So why the lack of sympathy for learners? If the language is to continue to thrive in any way then surely there will have to be a tolerance – indeed an encouragement – for learners. It's a mystery to me, forever an outsider of course, how the tightly closed-off Welsh-speaking world hopes to endure unless all are invited to attempt to share in the language. Why must the most frightening, the most intimidating part of learning Welsh be the fear of speaking it in public? And how strange not even to know who to speak it to! Do they speak Welsh or not? Will they speak it with a learner or not? The language conundrum.

Dydd Tri: Panic Is Upon Us

PANIC! My mind is a mental blank. Every phrase I've learned is suddenly out the window. I can't think! I'm with a new partner today, and her voice is shy, quiet, hard to hear in the babble of sound from the others in the room. But she is confident. She knows this stuff! My mind is a bubble of empty air. My heart races with anxiety as I see Rhys approaching. I don't even remember *Mae hi'n mynd – Mynd? Mae? Ydy?* Where was I when we did those words? Well, THERE of course (*wrth gwrs*) but I may as well have been asleep! *Cysgu*, to sleep. I can remember that. How do you say "to phase out"? That's where I am this morning, mentally phased out. Oh well, dive in anyway.

Mynd – mynd – going places, going SOMEWHERE, which I sure am not! "*Sai'n*", "I'm not". There, I remember that one. "*Sai'n mynd i unman.*" "I'm not going anywhere." I think that's right. IS that right? I'd like to go somewhere – right out the door! I'm overwhelmed. I want to run away. I give up. I throw in the towel. Hmm, there's an expression for you. How would one say THAT in Welsh?

Cocktail games. Everyone bumping around the room asking *enw* (name), or *gwaith* (job), or what did you do last night (*neithiwr* – last night). Now I have to try to use *mynd* and *ydy* and *mae hi'n* in sentences and I can't! I try to smile and stay calm but I'm a hopeless case. I feel eyes on me – "poor thing" – "brain dead obviously" – heads shaking. And I did my *gwaith cartre* last night too! But homework doesn't count for much now. It's no longer words on paper (*papur*), it's CONVERSATION. It's living words responding to spoken words and it's separating the puppies from the big dogs right now! I don't even feel paper-trained yet and here I am with experienced guard dogs!

Amser coffi – thank goodness! I stumble out the door and down the steps toward a strong cup of black coffee. I gulp air and fight down tears of frustration. I tell myself to calm down. I tell myself it isn't that important. But I know it is. I want to do this so badly, to speak Welsh. I walk around the campus focusing on purple hydrangeas with heads as large as cabbages, and bees drifting in and out of the flowers. I think of my little silver Fiat in the parking lot and managing to drive in the left hand lane shifting with my left hand. It steadies me. I breathe easier. I can drive on the left. I can learn this language of Welsh. Now I know it will be a slow process and it will be painful. It will take much, much time and effort. It will NOT be easy. It may well be the most difficult thing I have ever tried to do. But others have managed to do it and so can I.

I notice Angie, from Australia, standing in a patch of sunlight looking out towards the sea. She sees me and rolls her eyes, making a silent scream with her mouth. I smile. I'm not alone in my feelings. It is a profound revelation to me.

She approaches and says "I'm over my head here. It's hopeless! I haven't a clue what's going on."

Our frustrations pour out. The instructor is talking VERY fast. We can't remember yesterday at all. The morning WAS hard – a killer! With a sigh of relief that someone else is also floundering we shoulder the burden of returning to class for more. My mental block fades away and I suddenly feel clear-headed, determined to start anew.

New verbs. We repeat each sentence fifteen times and Unit 5 (*Uned Pump*) is off to a start. Only now am I ready to tackle it. I listen carefully, repeat, jot down notes, and it begins to make sense again. I've passed through my first panic attack and survived. Lunch comes before I know it, and two o'clock again before it seems possible. I feel opened again to possibilities and confident about what is happening in class.

Everything is now *yn y gorffennol*, in the past. From my lack of confidence to the tense of verb we spend the afternoon struggling with.

"This is MOST important stuff," Rhys tells us. " This must be memorized."

"*Es i, est ti, aeth e/hi, aethon ni, aethoch chi, aethon nhw,*" we repeat over and over with him.

It's *mynd* again, only this time it is "went", not "go". I can see that I won't go anywhere tonight. I'll obviously be wallowing in Welsh verbs and past tense of *mynd*. *Heno* – tonight. I sigh. *Heno* I study.

Dinner is quick, nibbled at my desk in my cubicle room while jackdaws perform their evening aerobatics outside my window. Notebook open in front of me, I sort through everything I have learned. This morning will never happen again! I make some quick vows:

1. I will eat breakfast in the mornings.
2. I will get enough sleep at night.
3. I will study every evening.

I will figure this stuff out before I sleep. *Cwsg* – sleep. Very tempting. But I give it the time it needs. I imagine the Welsh cocktail party for tomorrow.

"Beth wnaethoch chi neithiwr?"

What did I do last night? Well, I studied Welsh. That's all. Then I went to bed, the word *cwsg* running through my sleep.

Dydd Pedwar: We Are Speaking Welsh!

I went to bed at eleven last night (*neithiwr*) so today I am NOT *wedi blino*. No, not tired at all. I had *tost* and *sudd oren* for *brecwast*. It's amazing what a little toast and orange juice for breakfast will do for you! I am ready and prepared for class today, attitude positive and clearly focused. So how odd it is to get to class and hear Heather saying, "I have a mental block today. I can't remember anything I've learned!"

I look at her with great sympathy. I had visited that place yesterday and knew where she was. Meic looks at me and comments that he hopes class won't be so hard today. I agree. Visions of another Welsh "cocktail party", where I stand helplessly and mutely while others jabber the incomprehensible, flit through my mind. But it is worry for nothing. *Dim byd.*

As Rhys enters and sits down the sun breaks through the clouds and pours into the room. It is a prophecy for the day ahead. Revision is painless, even fun. We roll dice, we ask twenty questions, we cheat and look at our verbs. We gain confidence enough to put them away again, and daring enough to attempt to add nouns we know. We laugh and joke, and always Rhys is at our side to gently correct our grammar and pronunciation. We are surprised to know how much we have already learned – how much we really know.

The sun is out. *Mae hi'n braf.* It is fine in the sunshine on the steps, sipping *coffi* and tossing off Welsh words and phrases as if we owned the language. Laughter is high on the mild air. Today is full of *hwyl.* Fun.

After the break we learn the words for food (*bwyd*). Everyone is interested, everyone can relate. What had we eaten for *brecwast* that morning? Our list grows and grows. Nigel had *wyau wedi ffreio* with *sosejys* and *tost*. We can almost smell the fried eggs and sausage, hear the crunch of toast. Heather had *bara saim* and *madarch*. We can almost see the warm mushrooms being ladled onto the fried bread. It is almost *amser cinio*, and when so close to lunchtime the *bola* begins to rumble in hunger.

Caws, tatws, brechdan, cawl – everyone is ready to eat! Cheese, potatoes, sandwich, soup and anything else the mind can conjure. Before we can begin the conjuring we are already on to *te*, and visions of plattersful of *cacan* (cake), *tartan* (tarts), *hufen* (cream), and *pice ar y ma'n* (Welsh cakes). Somehow all the words are easy because we are so busily identifying with them all!

After the lunch break our thoughts turn from food to the weather. *Tywydd*. Each set of weather words flows easily from our lips until Rhys asks us to repeat a phrase.

"*So hi'n rhy wlyb*," he says, looking brightly at us and waiting for our response.

We have been struggling already with the "hr" sound he seems to give the *rh*. And here it is again in *rhy*. But *wlyb* puzzles us all. WHAT is he saying? We don't get to see the words first that we are repeating, just say them after him. And this *rhy wlyb* seems impossible! None of us has a clue what sounds to make that will approximate the word *wlyb*. We stare fixedly at his mouth, trying to see the shape of this strange word he is saying. Rhys suddenly stops and looks at all of us looking at him with such hypnotic concentration. Fifteen pairs of eyes staring at his lips.

"What are you all LOOKING at?" He blushes fiercely.

He is disconcerted enough to relent and writes *rhy wlyb* on the board for us. Mostly to keep our concentrated stare from his face, I think. Somehow we all manage to pronounce "*rhy wlyb*", trying to twist the "hr" sound around our stubborn tongues.

So hi'n rhy wlyb. It isn't too wet.

In fact, it is just the opposite as we are asked to now pronounce *rhy sych*. "Too dry." Each "ch" clicks out of our throats as a "k" sound, and Rhys repeats again "*rhy sych*" with a wet, throaty "ch". On it goes. Our non-Welsh-speaking tongue must learn to position itself in new ways and none of us is quite sure HOW!

At five o'clock Angie turns to me, eyes sparkling, and says, "It wasn't too hard today!" (*Rhy anodd* – too hard.)

It is true. Food and weather are easy things to talk about and remember and we have easily regained our lost confidence. Everyone walks out of the room smiling, and Meic says, "*Gwela i chi 'fory*". "I'll see you tomorrow."

We all venture a "*Pob hwyl*", or a "*Da iawn*", or at least a "*Ta ra*".

We are speaking Welsh!

Dydd Pump: Filled Up With Welsh

REVISION DAY and everyone approaches the classroom with grim smiles of doom and foreboding. How much on the spot will we be? How much do we remember? Anything at all? My head swims with words, searches for the phrases which will string them together. Everyone's faces look tired – *wedi blino* – and taut with apprehension. Still, there is also an element of relief here. After all, it is Friday! And we all realize how desperately we need this review. Today is our chance to make sense from the piles of rules and verbs which have inundated us for five days now.

We aren't put on the spot at all. We are put into groups of three and play a food-review game with a board and dice. What did you have to eat? *Ces i sŵp, ces i gyri.* We toss off the words for "soup" and "curry". It's easy and fun. Everyone is laughing.

Then we do a travel-question game in pairs. Pictures of places around the world. *Llundain, Sbaen, Groeg, Awstralia.*

Aethoch chi i (Have you been to)… London? Spain? Greece?,
Naddo, naddo, naddo. The Americans have not been anywhere!
Aethoch chi i New York? Montana? Arizona? California?
Naddo, naddo, naddo. The Welsh have not been anywhere!

The morning advances. "What is your name?" "Where do you live?" "Where did you come from originally?" "Do you work?" "What do you do?" "Where did you go last night?" "What did you do?" "What did you have to eat?" "What's the weather today?" Some things we can practically answer in our sleep by now, ask without thinking. "*Dych chi'n gweithio?*" "*O ble dych chi'n dod yn wreiddiol?*" Other things we struggle for, trip over, search frantically through our papers for a familiar guide to tell us where and why this word mutates, what it does in the future or in the past.

Then we are speaking it. It begins to flow off our tongues. Still sticking on *ch* and *r* and *rh* and *ll*, but flowing word into word. We are speaking from memory or from knowledge and new understanding, or both. An entire sentence and then another – IN WELSH!

By lunch all apprehension has gone. It has been vanquished by the games and laughter. We have been nourished by Rhys's gentle, supportive encouragement. We have almost completed our first week of Welsh.

Mae hi'n braf. It is fine outside, and a quick walk takes me to the National Library of Wales – *Llyfrgell Genedlaethol Cymru.* Standing on a hill overlooking Aberystwyth and the sparkling sea beyond, it is a perfect spot to eat lunch. *Heulwen.* A lovely word for "sunshine", and I eat my lunch in its warmth as I drink in the vivid blue of sky and sea. How good even the cafeteria turkey-salad sandwich tastes in the "*heulwen*" on a blue-sky day in Wales looking out at the sea! It's hard to leave and go back to the classroom once again.

Final revision activity – translation. We are surprised to learn that we can DO this! We realize that we can understand line after line, and someone comments that five days ago we knew NO Welsh. Now we have words we can read and say out loud, pronounce correctly and be understood. Maybe only by patient, sympathetic Welsh speakers. Maybe only the simplest of conversations. But the building blocks are now beginning to be put in place. We now have Welsh knowledge.

Rhys says to us, "You are being filled up with Welsh."

It is a foot in the door, a tiny crack through which we can begin to enter. I realize the work ahead. I realize it is only the beginning of years of study and struggle. But already so many puzzle pieces have come together. I understand so much more than I did before.

There are still moments of doubt. The "Am I insane?" questions still sweep over me at times. But I am hooked, because now I have the beginnings. I have the key to open whatever the door is I might be looking for. I have the beginning of being "filled up with Welsh".

Dydd Sadwrn: Bubble and Squeek

I listen to the *Eisteddfod Genedlaethol* as I dress this morning, broadcast live from the *pafiliwn roc*. I can understand about every sixth or seventh word if I'm lucky. I hear many, many words that I know I should know but can't quite remember what they mean. Still, I seem to get about a third of the contextual meaning of what I'm hearing. It's better than I could ever have hoped to do a week ago!

I look out the window. It rained in the night, a pleasant, gentle rain to sleep to, but this morning is mild and sunny. I have slept until nine o'clock, relishing every lazy minute in bed. I am a student again. Saturday is as sweet as I remember from distant college days. Today represents freedom!

The first challenge is finding a parking space in the downtown car park. I pull the little silver Fiat into a space and look around me. Across the street is a superstore complex which immediately repels me. I can see those anytime in America. I turn with the crowd of Saturday shoppers and head into the quaint and winding streets of Aberystwyth. It seems as if everyone in town is out on this humid morning. The narrow streets bulge with people carrying shopping bags. The *Siop Fara* is tempting with the fresh loaves of bread and cakes in the window but I pass by without stopping. The Woolworths, not far from the dingy-looking little *Plaid Cymru* offices, is my first destination. I need coat-hangers. Then down the street to browse in the big bookstore. I am disappointed here. Not much on Welsh or things Welsh. But a few blocks away I find a magical little corner *siop* full of things Welsh. In fact, it is all they sell. I spend an hour browsing through CDs and books in both Welsh and English and make several purchases. Then I cross the street and pass by a China shop with a window full of plates. In the middle of the window is a plate that catches my eye. Along the edge of the dish is the legend "Bubble and Squeak" in large blue letters. I had just heard this term a week ago in *Caerdydd* while visiting friends. They had told me about "bubble and squeak" being the meal they were always served on Monday, washing day, when they were children. It was a concoction of leftover Sunday's food, cabbage and onions and mashed potatoes, all fried together in a pan. They had asked me if I'd ever had it, and of course I hadn't even heard of it before. They had pitied me, telling me it was "just wonderful" and "a brilliant food". And now here is a "Bubble and Squeak" plate looking out at me from the window. I'm enchanted by it and have to go in to purchase it for my "bubble and squeak" friends in *Caerdydd*.

All this walking and shopping has made me hungry and I notice that it is almost one o'clock. There is a big, modern looking pub on the corner which seems to be full of a lunchtime crowd. I turn in and order a Guinness with my Ploughman's lunch, and spend an enjoyable half hour watching the people and listening to good Welsh *roc* music from the speaker system. So far the day has been a pleasant one but I still have to do my grocery shopping so, with regret, I leave the pub and return to the car park to retrieve my car.

The giant Safeway superstore to the south of town is larger than any Safeway I remember seeing in the U.S. Despite my misgivings about seeing things American creep into the Welsh culture I must admit to myself that this is a wonderful store for grocery shopping. What makes it an adventure, rather than a chore, is the novelty of seeing row after row of foods I never see in America, and often have never heard of before. This can also work in reverse, becoming an exercise in futility as I search for the familiar items I want but can't find in a Welsh Safeway. I am fascinated by the profusion of peas, and pea products. There is actually a can of "pease", really smashed peas, as in the old nursery rhyme "pease porridge hot, pease porridge cold, pease porridge in the pot nine days old". I didn't know what it was before this moment of seeing a can of it on the shelf! I am overwhelmed by the abundance of frozen fish, fish and chips, fisherman's pie, fish in sauces – more frozen fish products than I have ever seen. I am stunned by the variety of cheeses which must be purchased, cut to order, from a woman behind a counter. I have never seen so much curry and curry accompaniments in my life! But I can find nothing Mexican. What is a country coming to where you can't find the makings for *tacos* and *burritos* and *chimichangas?* Where can a refried bean and chilies *jalapenos* lover go? What about sour cream *enchiladas* and *carne asada?* And where are all the fruits and vegetables? I have to admire the lovely tomatoes in Wales, but how about artichokes and avocados? Where are the big ears of corn for corn on the cob? And watermelon? Just as I am about to despair I stumble down a frozen food aisle and am ecstatic to see a big frozen box of – "Bubble and Squeak"! I have to fight with myself to keep from clapping my hands and shouting "Yes!" Into my basket go two boxes of the magic concoction. Now I shall get to taste the "brilliant food" for myself!

I head back up the hill to the college with my bags of food where I unpack them into the refrigerator, then write some postcards and actually look at my Welsh for an hour before being lured by my Welsh purchases to play my new Welsh CD and attempt to read the *Tafod y Ddraig* I had bought. It is a struggle, but with the help of my dictionaries and my new knowledge of Welsh I can actually read some of the articles. I feel a sense of achievement that reinforces my desire to keep on learning.

Dinner at seven finds us at a warm, cosy Italian restaurant, which is a pleasant change from my own cooking in the dorm. The stone floor, the fireplace cheerfully burning, the red-checked tablecloths and Chianti bottles with candles, snugs us into a little world apart from the bustle of Aberystwyth's streets. Around us at the other tables people are speaking mostly Welsh. A dark-haired, ruddy-cheeked man next to us eloquently waves his hands as the Welsh words roll effortlessly off his tongue. I find myself looking at him in admiration of his easy fluency, but a quick glance from him reminds me that my look in his direction can be misinterpreted. He smiles. I smile and return my attention to my pasta. My glance falls on the empty gin and tonic glasses still on our table. I spend a minute on the nagging puzzle of Wales and ice. I had exactly two small chips of ice in that drink when it was served, barely enough to symbolize ice, let alone cool a drink! I wonder, with a smile, if there is an unwritten law somewhere in Britain about ice cubes. To my American mind it doesn't seem that ice cubes are a luxury – more of a human right! I vow that if I ever know a Welsh person well enough, I will ask about the ice mystery.

The Welshman at the next table doesn't seem at all perturbed by the lack of ice in his drink. He takes a complacent swallow and I avert my gaze lest it be misinterpreted again!

It is a perfect summer evening for Wales. The soft night air is actually warm and there is no wind along the seafront promenade. We join the crowds along the *traeth*, the beach, young and old alike out to enjoy *nos Sadwrn*. Ahh – Saturday night! Strings of white lights illuminate the walkway, and on the hillside the tram and it's track are also lit. The soft swish of the waves on the sand mixes with the chattering of Welsh from benches and clusters of family groups. A few groups of college-types laugh rowdily as they cross the street to visit yet another *tafarn*, but the entire atmosphere is pleasant and wholesome. Everyone is there to be out in the night air, to see friends and chat. The Welsh around me reminds me of birdsong in trees at twilight – chirpy, good-natured, and (sadly) unintelligible to my ears. It is one of those charming things I so love about Wales, the people so chatty, gregarious and lively and, above all, non-threatening. To Americans used to the violence of city streets and lack of trust of others on the streets at night, this little land where people extend courtesy and friendliness and seem to just enjoy each other's company, is charming above all else. My scant Welsh runs through my mind and I think to myself, *Mae hi'n noson braf*. It is a fine night and I wish it wouldn't end…

Dydd Chwech: This "language thing"…

I arise late, and one glance out the window causes me to scrap my plans of climbing up Constitution Hill or even taking the cliff railway up. The wind is blowing the rain slantwise in huge gusts, and the trees are bowing toward the ground. What happened to the perfect summer of last night? Ah well, this is Wales, and the weather is, as always, fickle. I decide to study my Welsh as I eat breakfast. But by eleven thirty I am feeling claustrophobic in my tiny cinderblock cell of a dorm room. Class doesn't begin until two o'clock so I should have time for a drive first. I had always planned to go up to the Cwm Rheidol on the little steam train, but today's weather doesn't make that an attractive option. Still, a drive up there in the car will suffice I decide.

I take my books and homework with me, in case the mood should strike to review, and go out to brave the storm. It is a pretty drive with very Welsh scenery. The grey rain clouds and drizzle only enhance the feeling of Welshness as I wind through green hills dotted with sheep. In the *cwm*, along the river valley, the wind tosses the branches of the old oaks and shadows fill the woods. It is exactly the kind of day I love in Wales. The hills and valleys seem timeless to me, as ancient as history itself. I stop to watch the sheep, oblivious to the rain, wandering the scrubby hillside or lying still as the ancient rocks around them. Far away at the bottom of the valley I can see a farm and a narrow ribbon of road winding to it. I am alone, or as the Welsh say "on my own" (*ar fy mhen fy hun*), but not lonely, not *unig*. I feel a part of this Welsh landscape that I love so much.

My mind returns to my immediate present and I remember that I have class at two. I remember also, as I drive back towards Aberystwyth, that today is the day we change *tiwtors*. There will be a new face at the front of the classroom when I get there. We all liked Rhys so much that the transition to a new tutor will be difficult. As I pull into the college parking lot I wonder what the new person will be like and hope for the best.

As I enter the classroom I sense a different atmosphere. Everyone smiles a little tightly. Apprehension is thick, almost tangible, and I notice that all eyes are turned to the board at the front of the room. A stranger's thin back with long, lank hair flowing down it is all I see. Like chicks too closely bonded to their mother, the class (the *dosbarth*) resists this new teacher. Our first exposure to Welsh came from Rhys. What might this stranger do to our thin and fragile confidence? Will we really learn as much from her? She turns around and smiles at us. It is a nervous smile, and I realize that she is aware of what being the second "*tiwtor*" in line means. She tells us that her name is Judy, and she is from *Gogledd Cymru* (North Wales). As she says this she spits facetiously and makes a hex sign, in imitation of what other parts of Wales does when they hear "North Wales". She has a sense of humour! Things start to feel better.

Then she begins to speak to us in Welsh! She fires it off rapidly and her dialect is not that of Rhys with his Mid-Wales pronunciation. Immediately my mind is grasping for any familiar word to try to make sense of what she is saying. To make it worse she is using new words and different spellings for words that we learned the previous week. We'd just begun to get them down and now this change! What does she mean by *eisiau*? Last week we learned *moyn* for "to want". What is this *licio*? We learned that *hoffi* means "to like". Why is she saying *rwy'n* when we know "I am" is *dw i'n*? Our frustration mounts as she talks.

We launch into an hour of revision of Friday's work – the ownership of things. We ask each other questions about these things and then she tells us to do it in past tense and in third person. Then follows a quiz on "yes" and "no", whose forms now number about six. We must decide if it is *do/naddo, ydw/nacdw, ydy/nacdy, oedd/nacoedd, oes/nacoes*, or just plain *ie/nage*. Our frustrations now amount to near panic. But before we have time to think about it we are on to a mutation drill – *d* to *dd*, *c* to *g*, *p* to *b*, *b* to *f*, *m* to *f*, and of course sometimes *g* disappears altogether. By coffee break I feel that sense of utter despair that I experienced the other day. How can I think I can ever SPEAK this language?

As I sit over my cappuccino I ask myself, "What am I doing here?" I think of the sheep-covered green hills that I had watched the rain fall on that morning. Surely this language thing isn't what I meant to do with a precious month in Wales! But as I stare out of the big windows toward wind-swept Cardigan Bay below me I realize that yes – of course it IS what I meant to do. I know that I love each new word and idiom that my mind can manage to retain, or "own" as I call it when I no longer ever forget the meaning of a Welsh word. Once I have it over and over and always know it I OWN it, it becomes mine, and there is not a better feeling of victory! This stuff is going real fast, and it is hard to "own" a lot at this pace. The young college kids are whizzing through the tenses and conjugations almost seamlessly. I don't think I have devoted enough time to it, I realize now. I don't "own" the mutations. I have no problem "owning" the *geirfa* – the nouns, verbs and adjectives. These come pretty fast for me. But I LIKE words. It's grammar I hate! I have been resisting this verb conjugation stuff which obviously can no longer be avoided. We can't always live in the present tense!

Around me whirls the chatter of coffee time. Holly from Pen-y-bont is talking about her parents' farm (*fferm*). She has lived on it all her life and parts of the stone walls in the farmhouse date back to 1570. She turns to me to ask a question about America. She wants to know why Americans allow such a violent gun culture to thrive. I have been asked this question before and it is always difficult to answer. I tell her there is no simple explanation for this ongoing problem, especially in America's schools. I admit that Wales seems like a much more wholesome country than America, and immediately all of the Welsh people at the table agree that it is. They seem pleased that I have recognized the charm of their country. Holly invites me to visit her at her parent's farm, and immediately gives me her address with that typical Welsh friendliness and enthusiasm I have come to so appreciate. It isn't really that they are friendly to just every person who drives down their roads, but once they know you for a reason (as in class), or through a friend's introduction, they are HUGELY hospitable and warm. How different from cool, suspicious Americans who never even speak to their neighbors!

After the break Judy begins a new unit, which is met with sighs of relief by the class. Now we are again learners, not reviewers, and no longer "on the spot" so to speak. There is no panic associated with learning something completely new because we aren't accountable yet. This lesson is about like (*licio* in North Wales, says Judy) and want (*eisiau* in North Wales, says Judy), with all the attendant nouns and repetitions aloud. Unlike Rhys, Judy is not into the 15 repetitions and individual repeating of each word or phrase. We are so used to this, to hearing our pronunciation aloud and Rhys' gentle prodding until we get it right, that we feel cheated. How will we ever get that all important pronunciation down this way? What will make the new words stick, semi-permanently at least, without those repetitions? Still, on the positive side, it is good to hear lots of Welsh being thrown at us as we really have to listen carefully to understand. Maybe something will stick after a day or two of this. We look at each other, reserving judgment for now. But at the end of the class there is much "eye rolling" as we pass each other. Or blank faces whose expressionless eyes say much – "Oh boy… " or "I miss Rhys… " or "So what do you think?" I wonder what I really think and decide that it is just "Well, onward we go – *cerddwn ymlaen.*"

Dydd Saith: To Keep the Language Alive

Today is one of those days – *Mae hi'n bwrw glaw ac yn wyntog.* It is windy and rainy. Much as I like that kind of weather I feel the greyness pulling me down. I have a trapped kind of feeling as I head out of the cinderblock cell to go to class. Maybe I'm dreading being put on the spot, even though I spent three hours sorting out my verb endings, mutations and "yes/no's" last night. I still don't have it all in my memory. I know I need to work more on it but something in me rebels at things grammatical! It's too mechanical, too analytical or something. I'm in love with the words themselves. I have this huge mental accumulation of words, but it is the process of learning to string them all together into sentences that is so difficult!

My partner this morning is Cerys, from Canada. She is *rhy ifanc.* Her mind is full of her weekend, what *tafarns* she visited, how much *cwrw* she drank. My mind is full of verbs and rules and I can see how dreary she finds that. We are reviewing ownership again, but the games are fun and it is easy – despite the hangover Cerys complains of.

Judy introduces the aspirant mutations and they are three strange mutants indeed. They warp and distend words as you try to change *p*'s to *ph (plant – phlant), t*'s to *th (tŷ–thŷ)*, and *c*'s to *ch (ci–chi)*. Things easily get to be *traed moch* (a mess!) with these words. We are puzzled how *traed moch*, literally meaning "pig's feet", can mean "a mess" but Judy assures us that it does.

Thinking that aspirant mutations are the worst of it is only wishful thinking we discover. We move on to the nasal mutations where every letter and word makes you sound like you're sneezing or ready to spit phlegm! *Fy nhrwyn*! *Nghaerdydd.* When *g*'s become *ng*'s it's almost as puzzling as when they disappear without a trace. When *t*'s aren't *t*'s anymore, but *nh*'s, and *p*'s are now *mh*'s, it's a confusing language for sure. And remember that it is consonants that cause this but never vowels. But if there is *ar* and *i'r* and *y* and *yr*, or *am* or *o* or *i* or *beth* then it all goes to soft mutation – ONLY if it is a feminine word however. No rule really exists for knowing what is feminine though, so it is all a matter of learning every feminine word in Welsh – now there is a cheerful thought!

As if all these mutants today aren't bad enough, we get another "no/yes" form. We are now at eight and still counting! Whatever happened to simple "yes" and "no"? In Welsh you do have *ie* and *nage*, but only in the present tense. And there is *do* and *naddo* but only in the past and only if a direct question has been asked. The *oedd* and *nac oedd, ydy* and *nac dy, ydw* and *nac dw, oes* and *nac oes* REALLY don't mean "yes" or "no" at all. They mean "I do" or "I don't", or "he does" or "he doesn't" etc. I notice with wonder that coming soon is *fydd* and *na fydd*, which is another "yes/no" which pops up in the future. My head reels with trying to keep them all straight! How will I ever truly remember which is which in real conversation?

By lunchtime I feel that hopelessness that I never again wanted to experience. Maybe it is the grey and gloomy weather. Or maybe all those mutations and "yes/no's". Whatever the cause, I am again questioning my sanity at the seemingly hopeless task ahead of me. The old question of "Why?" keeps surfacing. Why go through all this? Where will I speak it? Who will have the patience to listen to my attempts? I need someone to speak Welsh to me in a slow, clear and simple way. Who would do that? I reconsider the Welsh, sometimes so friendly, warm and curious. Sometimes they are also fickle, unhelpful, closed off and cool. "Clannish" I've heard others say. Is this just my mood or is it true? Am I a threat to their culture? I hope to think I'm not. I'm not an invader! I only want to speak the language. Isn't this an act of love for Cymru? Isn't it an act of devotion and loyalty to Welshness? It is a courageous act, really, to try to look through the crack in the door to Welsh-speaking Wales. The English-speaking Welsh treat you like you are crazy for learning Welsh and the Welsh-speaking Welsh condescendingly humour you – IF you're lucky. It's a tough hill to climb alone!

After lunch the sun breaks through the clouds and my mercurial mood zooms upward again. I love our new *tiwtor*'s North Wales pronunciation and her North Wales expressions. I love to listen to her very colloquial speech. It flows together and lilts, it LOVES the language it is speaking. Her tongue caresses the words, leaps and rolls and lingers on them, until I too yearn to speak that way. It is truly music to the ears with its exotic *r*'s and *ch*'s and ups and downs, the inflections completely foreign to stodgy *Saesneg* tongues! I realize that I have a love/hate affair with *Cymraeg*. It is in my heart and soul for some mysterious, inexplicable reason, and angry as I get at it sometimes, I can't lose it. I am terminally attracted to it for better or worse.

At the break I meet Ben, a Welshman from "the valleys" – the *Cwm Rhondda*. He speaks Welsh to me the way I have wished for, slowly and simply, so I can understand him. He uses words he knows I've had in class, and phrases that he knows I have learned how to recognize and answer. We converse for awhile, in this very simplified way, in Welsh! I feel guilty for a moment for my lunchtime thoughts but I also realize that Ben, too, is a learner. He is a very advanced learner, but he has gone through the process and understands the pain. He is elderly, one of *yr henoed* in Welsh society. He is bent at the shoulders, fuzzy wisps of white hair cover his ears. Bushy eyebrows hang over the rim of huge dark-framed plastic glasses through which his deep-set twinkly eyes shine out at me. He looks strangely formal in his dark trousers and white shirt, and he is so short that I must look down to catch the wry, humorous twist to his mouth.

We sit down with cups of coffee and he tells me he is going to speak English with me now. I feel relieved. My range of conversational Welsh has been exhausted. He tells me about the life of miners in the Rhondda before the 60s, and says that he is from the generation called "the lost generation" – that generation of Welsh people whose parents and grandparents, aunts and uncles, all spoke Welsh to each other but forbade their children to learn it. It wasn't spoken in their presence. They deliberately held the language back from their offspring. Schools forbade Welsh to be spoken in class and they were not even taught the words to *Hen Wlad Fy Nhadau*. As I listen to him I see that he loves having an enthralled audience. He is sharing his life reminiscences with me and I love to hear about it. I know about the history of Wales, but I have never before met a Welshman who is the direct victim of the horrible language prejudice of the early 1900s. I feel drawn to him. He is living history of this land I love, and the embodiment of all that has been so wrong with it. He has had to struggle for years in his old age to try to learn the language that should have been his by right. I look at his eyes, full of spirit and without bitterness, and think of those Welsh who deride the language, ignore the language, or are totally indifferent to being Welsh at all. This terrible, beautiful struggle to keep the language alive seems to me, suddenly, like a holy grail of sorts. I am proud of Ben, and proud of myself. It is a struggle worth the pain.

Dydd Wyth: Fear Is Upon Us

Diawl! Today we learn how to swear in Welsh – we are told that this is a reasonably bad swear word. *Diawledig!* Awful! I start to ponder this strange thing. That a combination of letters can mean something bad in one language but have no meaning at all in another. *Diawl.* It has no meaning to my English-speaking ear. It could mean anything – could be a disease. "You're suffering from *diawledig.*" "The treatment will be *diawl* for you." Could be food – "We are having *diawl* for breakfast." "My mother always serves *diawledig* for dinner." It just doesn't sound like something I would shout when I slam my thumb with a hammer! I KNOW what I would say, and *diawledig* doesn't quite fit the need! Neither does *diawl.* But this morning is enough to make me want to swear in Welsh.

When we came into the room this morning we were faced with another new *tiwtor* and were told that Judy is sick today. It has been a shock because we have just begun to adapt to Judy, and now this new person sits at the head of the table. This new person, Eleri, is not at all like Rhys OR Judy, and she speaks Welsh differently yet again! We are trying to cope, but I see frustration all around. She is trying too hard, and is obviously nervous at being a substitute. Somehow she has a condescending attitude toward us that is not going over very well. She is also speaking Welsh very, very fluently and at the speed of the Lone Ranger's silver bullet! She is trying to review our homework, but we are sitting here speechlessly staring at her. Our minds are racing to catch a familiar word, to make sense of anything coming out of her mouth. Everyone is looking wild-eyed at each other.

The new phrase for our day is *Mae ofn arna i* (literally meaning "fear is upon me"), and it literally is! From the first minute it is a scramble to keep our minds going forward with her. First we gallop through revision of *gwybod* and *nabod* (to know facts and to know of somebody). Then we do a five-yard dash through ages – *Mae e'n ddwy oed* (he's two years old).

I feel I would be lucky if I could speak as well as a two year-old, let alone understand as much Welsh! We plunge next into more *geirfa* – more words. *Mêl, peswch, ffliw* – maybe she is wanting us to sympathize with the absent Judy with words like "honey", "cough", and "flu". Finally she gives us the most beautiful of all Welsh words – *hiraeth*. That ineffable word of longing defines everything Welsh. And then *calon* (heart), where *hiraeth* stakes its claim.

Best to have ended there, but she immediately dives into "illness" (quite appropriately, I feel).

"*Mae pen tost 'da fi,*" she tells us. "I have a headache." (We all do at this point, I think).

"*Mae bola tost 'da fi.*" My own stomach is aching at the thought of racing through the language in fifth gear!

"*Beth sy'n bod arnat ti?*" ("What's the matter with you?") Well, I think I may have broken my head, Eleri. It seems to be crammed full of sawdust, verbs and nouns conjugating into a stew of frustration. I think I feel a swear word coming on. *Diawledig!*

Lunch cannot come soon enough for us and it goes by too fast. But a wonderful surprise, a miracle really, is waiting for us as we re-enter the classroom. Judy has returned like an answer to our prayers! She seems to no longer have an "illness upon her". Our smiles are huge and I doubt if she has ever felt so welcome. She smiles at us and looks at our faces, so full of fervent gratitude for her presence.

"*Hapus?*" she asks us.

We begin to tell her just how *anhapus* we have been and she listens patiently for a few minutes. Then, with another smile, she tells us we will start a new unit. Forget "health" now, we are onto "time". *Amser.*

Mae hi'n dau o'r gloch – or is it *ddau o'r gloch?* Isn't there a soft mutation after *hi'n?* We scrabble around in our notes trying to sort out our mutation rules while struggling with this cumbersome new way of saying "it's two o'clock". This fearsome language! So full of words shortened by apostrophes, of missing letters, of mutants, of "yes" and "no's" beyond counting, of infinite and never-ending rules!

Mae hi bron yn – it's almost – *amser* for class to end isn't it? Because *mae hi'n braf heddiw*. It's a fine day today and at *pump o'r gloch* we all plan to seek out the elusive *heulwen*, that sunshine we see pouring across the sea from the windows behind our tables. *Y môr*. The sea – is beckoning to us all.

We wander down along the promenade soaking up the rays. The touch of sunshine is such a rare commodity here in Wales. You feel like reaching out and pulling it to you, storing it away for a grey day. The ruins of the old castle on the hill catch the golden glow and the stones feel warm on my fingers. I sit to look out at the bay. It is too beautiful, the water sparkling with a million glints of light, a distant stretch of land just visible through a hazy fog bank to the north – *yn y gogledd*. There is a sculpture on the cliff beyond the castle ruins. A huge, bronze, full-breasted woman with long hair streaming behind her stretches her arms out yearningly toward the sea. Around her base are the names of Aberystwyth's war dead. It is a poignant evocation of *hiraethu* – that verb of longing and yearning.

The green hills around Aberystwyth are a contrast to the sparkle of blue water and busy buildings. It is too pretty, too mild and pleasant, too charmingly exotic to leave, but shopping, chores, dinner and *gwaith cartre* still await me. Tomorrow is a revision day and that can't be ignored. I sigh. By *saith o'r gloch* I will be back in my cinderblock cell.

Dydd Naw: Dim Gobaith Caneri...

I awake this morning with *geiriau Cymraeg* crowding out the *Saesneg*. It is as if my mind has no room for English words, being so thick with Welsh ones these days. They are all out of context with anything, just random words and phrases, drifting along the edges of my consciousness. When I went to bed last night I hadn't been able to think what the phrase for "I'm sorry" was. But when I open my eyes this morning the first thing I say out loud is *"Mae' ddrwg 'da fi"*. I say it aloud again as I open the curtains and close the window. *"Mae' ddrwg 'da fi."* Where did THAT come from out of the dark corners of the mind? *Pryd* is there now too. Possibly because it means *"a meal"* and it is time for *brecwast* and my *bola* is growling. But how can I explain *wedi ymddeol?* "I'm retired"? Why wake up thinking that one? Wishful thinking I suppose.

Last night I had been frustrated over the past-tense verb endings that I couldn't seem to remember. My mind had felt overloaded and scrambled by all of the new things stuffed into it in one class day. But now I am suddenly feeling focused and aware, words are filling my head just BEGGING to be spoken aloud and tried. I randomly mumble *llwybrau, rhieni, rhedeg, teulu,* and that most elusive word *hefyd* (not to be mixed up with *hyfryd* or *Hydref!*) I can look *hefyd* up in the dictionary over and over again and still can't remember it, still can't own it. I hear it used a lot, which makes it even more aggravating.

I grab my dictionary and thumb to *hefyd* once again. There are past fingerprints all over this page. *"HEFYD.* Either, also, besides." I say it loudly, as if the noise will somehow imprint this on my brain. "Either, also, besides!" With a sinking feeling I know that I will forget this again within five minutes. What is there about this word? I own *hyfryd.* It means "lovely" and it IS a lovely sounding word. I own *Hydref.* It is the month of "October" and "autumn". My favourite month. Easy to remember. But "also, either, besides"? How do I remember that?

Hoping to soothe my struggling brain I turn on the radio to BBC

Cymru. I count fifteen *hefyd*'s in the first ten minutes! This is obviously a word I must somehow remember! Either, also, besides…

Today is a "big deal" kind of a day here in Cymru. It is the total eclipse of the sun in Cornwall, and in Aberystwyth they expect a 75% eclipse. Unfortunately, as far as I can gather from repeated pronouncements of *cymylog* on BBC Cymru, the forecast is for cloudy weather today. This will block out the visual eclipse here.

As I walk to class I agree with the weather forecasters. It is indeed cloudy today. The sky is full of dark, ominous clouds and the sea is leaden and sullen looking. But our class is cheery from the start. For one thing , I am sandwiched between Mair and Haf. Mair has studied Welsh before and seems to know every verb and the various verb endings without a second thought. She has Welsh-speaking parents who live in England and who never once spoke Welsh in the home when she was a child. They basically looked down upon their own Welshness. Now Mair is determined not only to reclaim her heritage but also her language which they denied her. Her goal is to speak Welsh with her own parents. Haf is Welsh but her parents never learned the language. She had four years of Welsh in school and has a wonderful pronunciation from hearing it around her for many years. She can easily explain to me the "why" and "how" of the language. The other reason class feels so good today is that it is a complete review day. I will be able to sort out all of yesterday morning's *traed moch* – that mess we found ourselves in with our substitute tutor.

We start, again, with Time. We tell various times of the clock to each other until we can virtually do it without the urge to look at our notes. *Canol nos* – "midnight" or "middle of the night". *Canol dydd* – "noon" or "mid-day". *Hanner wedi* – "half past". *Chwarter wedi* – "quarter past". *Un o'r gloch, tri o'r gloch, deg o'r gloch.* We tour the face of Time. I decide that the single worst moment on the clock is "25". In either direction. It can never, ever be twenty-five after or twenty-five before the hour because who can actually manage to get out *pum munud ar hugain wedi un ar ddeg o'r gloch*? Isn't it MUCH easier to just say "twenty-five past eleven"? Sometimes English seems so succinct when faced with Welsh!

Translating with my two knowledgeable and experienced partners is both easier and more painful than with, say, Angie from Australia. Angie and I can stumble along together in our semi-clueless ways, fumbling for verbs and flipping subtly back to our notes and worksheets. With Mair and Haf I am carried along, each verb tense coming out right, effortless and confident. My own pathetic grasping for a word, tripping up on a mutation, flubbing a verb tense makes me feel like a pre-schooler learning to read. But the kind, polite help I receive from both of them soothes my ignorance. They inspire me to grab a verb and try it, and to my surprise it is correct. In my inspired state I vow (again) to LEARN those verb endings tonight!

Before we realize it *amser coffi* has arrived, and the long-anticipated eclipse is about to begin. For the past hour as we were working I had begun to notice that it was chilly, and finally really cold. Now, as I look outside, the dark clouds are more threatening and dreary than ever. I remember the eclipse. Daylight is fading and the temperature is dropping as if it were dusk.

With cappuccinos in hand, we stare at the television set in the dining room, while the grey gloom deepens outside the big windows. The jackdaws grow noisy and restive, thinking twilight is upon them. But the thick cloud cover refracts too much light, diffuses it, and keeps real dimness from being very dramatic. With matter-of-fact acceptance the Welsh shrug and utter the new expression we had just learned from Judy before the break. *Dim gobaith caneri...* or "Haven't a canary's hope... ", which Judy told us referred to the canary that the miners would take into the mines with them. If the canary keeled over the miners knew that the oxygen level in the mine was low and they had to get out quick or they hadn't "a hope in hell". Today, the eclipse in Aberystwyth was suffering the same fate.

The mood is actually jolly after lunch. A sense of *hwyl* is upon us. Revision games, an eclipse, and now – a visitor! True, it is a salesperson making a blatant pitch for new subscriptions to her magazine, but it is a magazine in Welsh at various learner-levels so our interest is high. And, she speaks *yn araf* – slowly – in Welsh so that we are able to understand. With amazement I realize that I can probably get over 70% of all that she is saying. I know that I'm not exaggerating when she quizzes us (*yn Gymraeg*) at the end of her presentation and my partner and I only miss one question.

My amazement at my language-understanding abilities is reinforced when we play a revision translation game where we must read, remember, spell a paragraph for our partner, and then translate the paragraph. We spell every word correctly, understand each other perfectly and easily sail through the translation correctly. I do stumble on a few verb endings, and once more make my ongoing vow to LEARN them this very night!

Coffee break is lively, with lots of discussion about Welsh books, nationalism, Welsh history and Welshness, Welsh book sources, helpful Welsh websites and everything the obsessive-compulsive Welsh learner longs to know. I look around at this strange mix of people. All of them are bright, educated, interested in Celtica, many of Welsh heritage, many not from Wales. Many are young, some are middle-aged, a few are elderly. But MOST are not Welsh, in the sense of being born in Wales and thinking of it as the land of their fathers. It is probably the nature of this month-long intensive course to have such a composition. Who, except students, vacationers and retired people, can take four weeks off to learn Welsh? Although the Welsh in our class are being paid and encouraged by their employers to learn the language. I imagine that the ongoing weekly Wlpan classes offered all over Wales might have more Welsh people in them. I fervently hope so! I so much want to believe that the Welsh themselves are this interested in all things Welsh. I realize, however, that this is not necessarily the case and ponder the strange phenomenon of foreigners caring more about Wales than some Welsh people. Is it, as the American essayist Emerson once said, that "every ship is a romantic object except that on which we sail"? Or is there another, more insidious, explanation?

The day ends with another board game with groups of four in a team. The board square asks us to do various things. One square commands us to say time, another to use a past tense. It is VERBS all over the board, and by the end of the game I know that I will have to have a very VERB-al evening. I just can't ignore it anymore. I walk out of the door vowing yet again to be able to say (and mean it), "I actually learned my verbs last night!"

Dydd Deg: A Brotherhood Of Welsh Learners

With a shock I realize that I've barely thought about my life beyond Welsh class and Wales for two weeks! There just isn't any time left in the day to think beyond the immediate moment. The Welsh Class has become an entity unto itself. The people in our class are now such friends, so bonded, that we seem to be one unit with one fixed goal – *dysgu Cymraeg.* To Learn Welsh. Life that extends out past class time becomes centred around *gwaith cartre* – homework. If there's any free time left over it becomes a Welsh activity, or a form of physical exercise to counter so much sitting. There seems to be no other life! Mair comments on that very thing this morning as we cook *brecwast* in the kitchen. She says that it is the most restful vacation she has ever had because there is no time to remember work or have to feel stressed about the job. Of course for Mair, with her knowledge of Welsh already, there IS no stress attached to learning Welsh. But that fantastical sense of separation from other realities seems to be the case for all of us. For the moment it is all about Welsh.

Class today is fun. More *hwyl!* I have good working partners and everyone's mood is light. Everyone feels good and is healthy, a change from earlier in the week when some had a cold. No more boxes of the communal tissues on the table for runny noses. No more cough drops being passed around. Everyone is smiling, and Judy is in a gentle, playful mood that encourages our learning. We play some review games that make us noisy and giggly. We are kids today, no matter what our age. Then we do a translation, and because I really DID learn my verb endings last night I sail through all of it feeling proud of myself because I understood – AT LAST– the basis of this language we spend our days living with. Now I know I must just make myself learn things right away, so I am not straggling along, feeling one step behind.

Everything seems clear today. Numbers and time are easy and review games for these feel more like play than work. We learn new patterns of using verbs, new "constructions" Judy calls them. "We are", "we are not", "we have", "we haven't", "they are", "they aren't". *Dyn ni'n, so ni'n, dyn ni wedi, so ni wedi, maen nhw'n, so nhw'n.* Did we get those down right? Even this new stuff seems straightforward and understandable. Each thing we do is greeted by Judy with a warm *"Da iawn!"* There is something about the way this *da iawn* is said that doesn't seem to have an equal in English. Our much colder "very good" doesn't have the same fervour with which Welsh imbues *da iawn.* Even her sprightly little question *"Pawb yn hapus?"* rings much warmer and more musical than the English "Everyone happy?" And yes, everyone IS *hapus.*

The weather today is *braf,* so fine that it hurts to think what the eclipse would have been had it occurred today rather than yesterday. No clouds today, just blue sky and *heulwen* – brilliant sunshine that strikes points of dancing silver on the sea. It is a day that invites an outing and lunchtime is the perfect chance to take one. A quick drive to town in the Fiat and fifteen minutes to find a car park with an empty space. Lunchtime is being gobbled up by the busy streets of Aber. I finally find a spot to park and cross to the SPAR on the corner. A cheese baguette and a cold drink in hand, I decide to eat lunch sitting on the sea wall of the promenade. It seems that everyone else in town has the same idea. All along the way people are sitting on the wall, legs dangling over the beach below. We all stare out to the horizon, munching our sandwiches and gazing at the seagulls who push and squawk at each other down in the sand, each hoping for a crumb of baguette. On the beach several toddlers build mounds of sand and bury their feet in it. It is a very European scene to my American eyes. None of this is like anything I would see in America. No greasy fast food bags of French fries and burgers. No paper cups and straws. No skaters, no bikinis, no "druggie types". No fancy cars or expensive seafront restaurants and condominiums. No "boom boxes" shattering the noontime peace with rap music. Just FAMILIES, which I suddenly realize one would never see on a noontime Thursday in the American work world. Families playing in the sand, lying in the sun, chasing dogs in the sea, eating sandwiches and feeding the pigeons. Up on the gentle green hillside the little train car chugs its load of passengers towards the 'camera obscura' on top. I love it all, the wholesomeness, the peacefulness, the Welshness of it. I don't want to leave it, but I still have to retrieve my car and get back to class before the next unit begins relentlessly at two o'clock.

Uned 18 – Y Ffôn. Talking On the Phone. Here is something we can all relate to. Half of us have our cellular phones with us right now! Lots of new phrases here and lots of laughter and joking, lots of role playing of phone conversations in Welsh.

"*Alla i siarad â Ffred?*" "Can I speak to Fred?"

"*Na allwch, mae'n flin 'da fi.*" "No you can't, I'm sorry."

There is lots of help from Judy and more laughter. Everyone is focused completely on this task of phone conversations. And everyone is doing it all in Welsh! Up on the board Judy writes eight sentences in Welsh. In amazement I realize that I can read them all with complete understanding! Then she puts up eight sentences in *Saesneg* and we must translate them into *Cymraeg*. This is easy. I can do all eight. This is it! This is how it feels to know a little Welsh.

Dw i'n deall! I understand!

I can speak it! Not very fast, not very much, but I can DO it! This knowledge, in a sense this first real proof that we are actually learning, elates all of us. It has now been almost two weeks. Are we where we should be? Should we know more? Is that even possible in two weeks? All we know at this point is that we can speak and understand some Welsh. It is all we need to know for now!

Tonight is a splurge in celebration of our accomplishment. Mair says that the Tandoori restaurant at the end of the pier is excellent and we decide that we have been thrifty. We deserve this night out. We have worked hard and now we will reward ourselves. The restaurant is exotic and full of wonderful aromas. The windows face Cardigan Bay, west into the sunset – *y machlud*. A *peint o gwrw* while we browse the menu, then a table facing the sea. We dip our Nan bread into yogurt and cucumber sauce, the spicy thali dinner. Then frozen lemon sorbet. We are finished just in time to get to the Welsh class *noson hwyl* at the *tafarn*.

It is one of those miraculous Welsh summer evenings when the air stays warm, the weather stays dry, the sky stays clear and the faint outline of the moon prepares for darkness. There are about twenty-five students sitting in a semi-circle of chairs on the patio of the pub. Chatter, laughter and beer – even a smattering of Welsh from the more advanced-level students. Nigel is there, and Holly and Beth, and Telor who grew up in Aberystwyth. Old Ben with the big black glasses sits across the lawn, his white eyebrows wiggling up and down as he tries his Welsh. There are six of us from our class, our class *grŵp*. Judy sits cross-legged on the grass, her back to the wall, with a guitar across her lap. Outside of the classroom she seems much less confident of herself, shy and quiet, a waif with a pinched-looking little face. But she smiles to see that so many students from "her" class have shown up. There is a real sense of comradeship here. We are a little society of Welsh learners, here to practice what we know with games and fun. First it is charades, with Welsh words and only Welsh allowed to be spoken. The words are kept simple and spoken slowly. Everyone gestures, laughs wildly, pounds their team members on their backs. Every time someone guesses correctly, in Welsh, they get a warm "*Da iawn!*" from the tutors. It is that wonderful *da iawn* that makes you feel you've accomplished a miracle because you've spoken words in Welsh. Our *grŵp* wins the charades game to our amazement. Judy picks up her guitar and passes out papers with words to Welsh songs on it. "*Sosban fach*" and "*Merch Megan*". She strums the tunes and we recognize them. We stumble once through the unfamiliar Welsh words, laughing at our ineptness. The second time we manage the words. The third time we sound like we are all singing in Welsh, and that spirit of camaraderie sweeps over us. We are a brotherhood of Welsh learners joined by our love for Wales. The moon is no longer a faint outline. It now fills the dark sky with a bloom of yellow light...

Dydd Gwener: You Don't Speak Welsh…

I awake this morning as if to Christmas morning. It is a most special day. This is the day I get to hear Dafydd Iwan sing in Porthmadog. The rain is beating on the roof of the dorm room and the wind is tossing the tree tops around in frantic circles, but nothing can dim the prospect before me. I have never heard Dafydd Iwan in live performance and he has been my personal hero for some time now. As I gaze out of the window at the grey and sodden morning my mind drifts back to my discovery of his music and the consuming need to understand what his message was to Wales. This, indeed, was the compelling force behind my learning Welsh. In the process of trying to decipher the Welsh words in Dafydd Iwan's music I became drawn to the language itself. In the dawning awareness of his importance to the Welsh culture and continuation of the Welsh language, of the very words he sang to his fellow Welshmen, I found my own blossoming admiration of the Welsh and their desperate race against time to save their Welsh culture. The more I knew about the language situation in Wales, the more the question burned to be asked – why only give the message to those who spoke Welsh? Why not to everyone in Wales? Why sing ONLY in Welsh, in other words, when so few in Wales could understand it? This question finally led me to write a letter to Dafydd Iwan the previous December, asking him to explain his rationale for singing in Welsh.

Standing here at the window I think back to the letter he wrote in response to mine. His explanation to me was clear and full of the passion that fills his music:

> … [you ask] why I seem to communicate only in Welsh, and do not even bother to provide translations into English, thus depriving the majority of Welsh people of the opportunity to understand my message. This is a dilemma which I have lived with for most of my life, and it is not easily resolved. Indeed, my attempts at explaining it may seem lame to you, but that may be inevitable!

The main reason why the Welsh language is in a stronger position than any other Celtic language today is that it has maintained a degree of independence. It can stand on its own feet, as it were, and be the medium for a total culture which does not have to be translated. Any language which is to have a chance of survival in this world of mass communications and uniformity has to maintain this degree of independence, of "separateness", if you like. Thus the 38-year campaign of Cymdeithas yr Iaith has been conducted largely through the medium of the Welsh language itself. The world is not aware of it, but it has certainly worked in Wales. For the people we really had to change their attitudes were, first and foremost, the Welsh speakers themselves. Singers (and artists using other media) such as myself used Welsh as our language because it was the natural thing to do. The fact that we only used Welsh was a part of our message, that *yr iaith Gymraeg* had an existence, and a dynamic, of its own. The medium was the message, in a very real and practical sense. Before the 60s, Welsh was the language of history, and of all things dying and decaying. We had to make it the language of the future, of youth, and of all things modern.

The question you now ask is whether we should now, speaking from a position of comparative strength, and having succeeded in our initial aim of changing the "mind-set" of the Welsh-speakers, endeavour to widen the scope of our message, and explain our mission to the wider public in Wales and beyond. The answer, without doubt, is "yes", but old habits die hard!

I think of his ardent belief that Welsh become the language of the future in Wales, and think of myself – standing at a window in a dorm room in Wales, having come all the way from California to learn Welsh, and of all the others in the Wlpan programme, indeed, of all the courses being offered all over Wales at this moment. I smile to think that there is hope that Welsh will truly BE the language of Wales in the new century. I think of the difference Dafydd Iwan, and others of his ilk, have made in Wales and I am filled with admiration for their dedication and faith. I think, also, of an interview with Dafydd Iwan that I had read, in which he stated that one of the things he hated (*cas bethau*) was *Cymry difater*, or indifferent Welsh people. The weakness of Wales is the indifference of so many Welsh to the language and culture. Despite all of the leaders who fight for the language, these *Cymry difater* hold the fate of Wales in their hands. Their attitudes, too, need to be changed.

The rain pelts the window with hard drops and I am brought back to the moment. There is a long drive ahead of me to Porthmadog in this weather, and I imagine how soggy the rugby field will be tonight at *Miri Madog*, the name given to the *roc* marathon where Dafydd Iwan would be singing. I ponder the name for a minute. *Miri Madog. Madog* is obviously short for Porthmadog, but *miri* means merriment and fun. Only in Wales, I think, would a rock concert be called *Miri!* I remember American rock concerts, with their drugs and violence, and hope that *miri* truly describes tonight's event.

We have planned to leave by eight o'clock, and I am missing class today for the *mawr* event in Porthmadog (as Radio Cymru bills it). As we drive I recall Julie's expression *Mae hi'n bwrw'n drwm* for "raining heavily", and the rain sounds like a drum on the roof of the car. The further north we get the heavier it seems to rain. The hills and oak trees are obscured by sheets of grey water gushing down the windows and we seem to be the only travellers on the road. Still, we reach Porthmadog in three hours despite the weather.

The streets of Porthmadog are clogged with traffic, and the sidewalks crowded with tourists bundled into rain gear or under umbrellas. By the time we manage to find a place to park, slog through the sheets of rain, find accommodation for the night and eat a quick lunch, it is well into the afternoon. We decide we should probably find out where the *mawr* event tonight is being held. We see a few small signs posted to light standards pointing with red arrows to "*Miri Madog*" so we attempt to follow them, turning down one road after another until we lose the signs altogether. So, we return to where we first saw the signs and begin again, thinking we must have missed something somewhere. Down a lane and onto a busy main street. More traffic jams and inching along. Down another road, and we are back at the same signs again! We are beginning to get frustrated now. A third time we slowly follow the arrowed signs, looking to our right and left carefully for any sign of the rugby field, and we finally see the sign we missed the first two times, pointing down a little side street. The street becomes a one-car mud-and-gravel lane, but ahead we see a huge, colourful tent (*pabell)* being erected in a soggy green field of grass. We have found the elusive spot!

Content that we now know where we are going tonight we drive out the Lleyn Peninsula towards Cricieth. The rain is still coming down, but not in sheets anymore. The imposing hill with the ruins of Castell Cricieth upon it looms out of the drizzle and we decide to get out and see it. It is an easy climb up a paved path and we have the castle to ourselves. The wind blows the rain in our faces as we stare out to sea, and I imagine the days when Llewelyn Fawr stood here on the ramparts of his castle. It is just a shell now, and I try to visualize doors and shutters over the gaping holes in the stone walls, firelight and candlelight where darkness and empty space now reign. It is not easy to span the seven hundred-year gap in time, but there is a magical quality to it all – our aloneness in the rain with Prince Llewelyn's castle.

Evening is upon us, and back in Porthmadog we look for a place to eat dinner. This is not as easy as it sounds, for it is only six o'clock and few places are open yet for evening meals. We find a very crowded little *tŷ bwyta* filled with others who can't wait until seven to eat. It is unremarkable except for the huge bowls of vegetables served with the tepid slice of roast beef. Carrots, roast potatoes and leafy green chard are fresh and wonderful.

Back outside it has grown chilly. We pull on sweaters when we reach the car. The rain has finally stopped, but dampness hangs everywhere in the evening air. The little road to the rugby field is full of teenagers heading towards the large tent in the wet grass. There are very few cars, which, to American eyes, is amazing. I think of a rock concert in America where the teenagers WALK! It is impossible to envision. But I realize that the driving age is different in Wales, and so is the economic status of teenagers. It is to be the first of many amazing discoveries about Welsh youth this evening. At the entrance to the *maes parcio* (car park) there is a man in a green vest who looks grateful for a car to direct. Thinking of the several groups singing tonight we pull up and ask him what time Dafydd Iwan will be singing. It is not really our intention to join the herds of teenagers for all of the evenings groups. I am there to hear Dafydd Iwan. The green-vested man tells us, "About ten thirty or so he performs". That gives us a lot of time to kill.

The mist is beginning to rise from the mountains in the distance, and we drive down to the marina and walk around looking at the boats. The red dragon of Wales (*y ddraig goch*) waves proudly from many of the masts. A few defiantly fly the skull and crossbones of the Jolly Roger. An occasional Union Jack is seen. I wonder if this mix is symbolic of the mix of people in the Porthmadog area. Around nine o'clock we head back to the rugby field where *Miri Madog* is in full bloom.

There are only around twenty cars in the *maes parcio*. I find myself wondering if the weather had something to do with a low turnout. But this is Wales! Surely rain doesn't affect anything! We wade across the flattened, soggy grass to the *pafiliwn* (pavilion). The rumble of bass guitar can be heard clear out here. The bar at the end of the tent seems to be filled with young people, but inside the main tent there are only a few clusters of teens really listening to the music. The grass has been worn to a muddy pulp around their feet. A group on stage is desperately performing and the massive speakers carry the sound in a deafening tremolo.

We step outside to save our ears and warm up with a cup of *coffi* from the refreshment stand. The woman behind the counter has no coffee made, obviously not expecting to sell any in that adolescent crowd. But she makes some for us, looking at us with a friendly, but very curious, gaze. When we open our mouths to speak we may as well be wearing big signs that say "AMERICANS". My jeans and boots have been getting the once-over from the teenage girls, and I wonder if Welsh women just don't wear things like that. We are obviously NOT adolescents. And I guess we are also obviously foreign looking. It is the first time I realize that.

We sip our coffee and wonder at the concept of having beer sold at a rock concert for teens. In America it would be an outrage if anyone proposed doing that. But in America the legal drinking age is 21 and in Wales it is 18. And what happens in America is that alcohol is smuggled in, along with drugs, and the event becomes an excuse for excesses. Drunkenness, fighting, violence in other forms, and getting high on drugs. The music either feeds the frenzy or becomes irrelevant. Here, despite the pints of beer being hoisted and downed, everyone seems to be in control, pleasant to each other, just sociably enjoying the music. There is no sign of drugs. It is innocuous, an almost wholesome feeling.

While pondering on these things we suddenly notice a little woman in a green vest approaching us. Short, chubby and matronly looking, she produces a glossy programme (*rhaglen*) and waves it at us. She asks if we would like to purchase one. We say "no". Our American accents immediately start the "AMERICAN" sign flashing in her eyes.

"You're American then?" she asks, already suspecting the answer. I nod. "Yes."

"What brings you to this?" Her eyes are bright with curiosity now.

"I came to hear Dafydd Iwan sing." I can see that this response increases the curiosity in her eyes.

"How do you know about Dafydd then, all the way in America?" She pronounces "Dafydd" with a proprietary air that seems to say he is a cultural belonging, as if she were talking about *Yr Wyddfa* (Mt. Snowdon) or Caernarfon Castle.

"I've read about him. I know all his music." This seems to amaze her.

"Really now? Do you? Have you met him then?" This seems to be a natural assumption on her part.

I smile at the thought and say, "NO, I've never met him."

"Would you like to?" Her bright eyes look at me with high expectation. She is about to bestow a gift.

I look at her in stunned amazement. Would I like to meet Dafydd Iwan? No! Yes! I can't imagine it. What would I say? I shake my head and say "NO!"

She refuses to take this as an answer. "Oh, but you must! He's around here, I just saw him. I insist! I'll be right back then." Before I can demure she is off, vanishing into the shadows of the rugby field.

I look after her. I laugh and shake my head. How very Welsh she is. I'm not sure what to think. Is she serious? I scoff at the idea. What would I do if she were serious? I can't even begin to imagine. But before many minutes pass I realize I'm not going to have to imagine. She is back, taking my arm and patting it in a motherly way.

"Come with me then dear. He's over here in his car. He'll say "hello" to you." She pulls me toward the dimly lit parking lot in front of the rugby club office. Everything is a daze to me. The shadowy parking lot, the dark stationwagon (estate) under the pale security light, the chunky little woman at my arm, the short man rising out of the car and reaching out to shake hands with a friendly smile. I recognize his face from countless CDs and videos. It is Dafydd Iwan. The little green-vested woman passes me off to him, a smile of pleasure on her face. She is so very casual about it – presenting me this way to George Washington, Abraham Lincoln, Llewelyn Fawr, God. The stunned disbelief on my part couldn't have been greater if it had been any of the above. And my stunned disbelief, I see, is now reflected on the face of Dafydd Iwan. He has said something. I haven't responded. The smile fades from his eyes.

" You don't speak Welsh." It is flat, monotone, a statement of fact.

" No I don't." It is the single worst accusation and the single worst admission I can imagine at that moment. It is a defining moment, really. I don't speak Welsh. Can there be anything worse here in Gwynedd, the heart of Welsh-speaking Wales? Can there be anything I wish I could do more? And can there be anything I want to admit less to this man, of all men? I was learning to speak Welsh. Yes! But at this moment none of the two weeks worth of Welsh I know will surface. I stand accused and guilty. I also lose all sense of good manners. He is looking at me in a puzzled way.

"You're American then?" That accent again.

"Yes," I nod.

"Whereabouts in America are you from?"

"California." I stand like a stone, barely aware of what I am saying. You don't speak Welsh!

The puzzled look deepens on his face and he leans forward against the car door impatiently. He is not used to a nameless stone staring at him in near-silence. "Have we met before?"

" No." Embarrassment floods over me. I haven't even introduced myself! Inanely I hear myself saying, "But I did write you a letter once."

His eyes sharpen into focus and he looks closely at me. "When?" he asks intently.

"Last December… "

Even more intent upon me now, he finally asks that which I should have told him long ago. "What's your name?"

I tell him my name and he continues to stare at me, eyes deeply thinking. Slowly, as if thinking aloud, he says, "You asked me for (the words to) '*Rhywbryd fel nawr*'".

I am amazed that he remembers. I did ask him for the translation to that song. He is still looking at me in that attitude of deep thinking.

"I wrote to you. I sent you that." He quickly shoots me a glance, squinting in concentration. "You did get that didn't you?"

I nod my head. "I did get it and I really appreciated it." He looks intently at me again, perhaps trying to decipher my American accent. After all, Nigel has told me I have a "drawl". I suppose that my " really appreciated it" sounds more like "rilly 'prishated't"

The long look continues, and then he looks down and says, softly and almost to himself, "I quoted from that letter several times."

He had told me that in the letter he had written to me. Now is my chance to ask what it was that I had said that so compelled him to quote me. But all rational sense of reasoning is beyond me here in the dimly lit parking lot of a wet rugby field in Porthmadog face to face with Dafydd Iwan. He is smaller than I had imagined. His voice is soft-spoken and Welsh accented. He is trying hard to make conversation with the semi-idiot I have become. He settles himself against the side of the car and smiles.

"Are you here on vacation?"

All I can think is how surprising that he said "vacation" rather than the British "on holiday"! I tell him that I am studying Welsh in the Wlpan course in Aberystwyth. We discuss the course for a few minutes. It goes on from there, his questions and my answers. "Who's running that course now?" "Did you go to the Eisteddfod?" Polite conversation with a total stranger. His graciousness, my shy responses. I feel intrusive, but he is trying hard to put me at ease. He leans across the open car door and suddenly says, as if it were something he just had to do:

"The gate steward told me that Americans were asking for me."

I am stunned by this. That the man at the *maes parcio* had told him we had asked about him was too hard to believe!

"We weren't 'asking' for you," I explain. "We just wanted to know what time you were singing."

He nods, thoughtfully, and says, "Well yes, that's what he said. That's what I meant."

I find myself wondering why it matters. Aren't we allowed to do that? Is it really such a singular thing to do? Those accents again – that Americans would be there and ASKING about Dafydd Iwan must have made an impression on the parking attendant! That he would pass it along to Dafydd Iwan seems even more singular. It shows me how close-knit a community we have stepped into here. This is certainly *Cymro Cymraeg* territory and we are the anomaly. Yet in no sense are we made to feel unwelcome. Just noticeable in the extreme!

"I just wanted to hear you sing, not the other groups." I feel the need to keep explaining.

He smiles wryly, and slides his gaze off towards the tent where the sounds of the rock group *Anweledig* can be heard. "This *Miri Madog* is an experiment. I have no idea how it will turn out. It is an act of courage for each of the groups singing to try to make it singing only in Welsh. This event is to show them that they can DO it, to give them confidence to keep trying. It is an incredibly daring enterprise to try to compete with English-speaking groups, although Catatonia has made it on the international scene."

I can sense his passion for the subject, for the "daring enterprise" and the "act of courage". It is pure Dafydd Iwan. He has shown me the entire production in a new light. One that has not occurred to me. I am here at what, essentially, is a continuing act of Welsh nationalism. Defiant of Wales to the world, these singers (for whom Dafydd Iwan set the role model) are not just there to sing. They are there to sing in Welsh. Therein lies all the difference.

I thank him for giving me his time and make my way back to the tent. *Anweledig* has drawn a larger crowd and the tent poles vibrate from the reverberation of the huge speakers. Suddenly the flow of Welsh words breaks into English and for a minute I can understand. "One nation, two languages", the lead singer scorns through the microphone. I look with profound interest towards the stage. "*Un genedl, dwy iaith*" – the language battle rages on.

Before I can think much about this interesting song a young girl approaches me with a stretched out notepad and pen. She informs me that she is from the *Porthmadog Press*, which I assume is the local newspaper. She is writing an article on *Miri Madog* and would like to get the impression of an American. My jeans? My haircut? I haven't really opened my mouth, it can't be the accent! I can't hear her over the blast of music, so we step outside the tent.

"What do you think of this event?" she asks brightly, eyes looking expectantly at me.

What do I think? I haven't really given that a thought. I think of the lack of cars in the parking lot, and the small clusters of teenagers listening inside the tent. I think it is profound that even *Anweledig* writes a rock song about Wales and the division of language and culture. I think it is kind of sad that not more people are here.

"I thought it might be more crowded than this. In America, if you had five big groups playing, it would be packed." I feel like a traitor, somehow, but it is what I am thinking.

She agrees with me about the lack of crowd and asks why I am there. Since I'm obviously past my teen years this is a logical question, but she is very tactful. I tell her I came to hear Dafydd Iwan. That seems to reassure her. I am obviously closer to that generation.

"I saw you talking to him in the parking lot." She looks curiously at me now, ready for anything.

"I just met him for the first time," I explain.

Her eyes glimmer and she smiles. "Is it exciting do you think?"

She has been busy jotting in her notebook and pauses now for my answer. I'm not at all sure what she wants. Is the rock event exciting or was meeting Dafydd Iwan exciting, or some other nebulous meaning?

"Well, it is all very interesting. Quite different from America." I waffle around searching for a safe, inoffensive answer. I am telling her the truth. It is like a country fair without the rides and cotton candy. It is like a rodeo without the cowboys but lots of beer. It is not like a rock event, but it is like Wales. It is small, it is not very well attended, it is damp and cold in the draughty tent. But it is truly a *mawr* event. A huge event. It is the Welsh language struggling to make it on its own terms. It is youth speaking, thinking, and singing in Welsh. It is a celebration of Welshness.

As we talk I notice that the audience is changing. It is becoming more diverse. I now see people who are obviously middle-aged and I realize that a different generation is starting to arrive. There are now more people here and the pavilion is starting to feel crowded in the front near the stage. *Anweledig* finishes their last number with a flourish of noise and cheers. The girl reporter for the *Porthmadog Press* gets what she wants, thanks me and moves away into the shadows. There is an indefinable sense of excitement in the air, of expectation, and a group of older women push past me with a huge Welsh flag under their arms. More teenagers now ooze into the crowd, sloshing dark beer from their pint glasses. Then, quietly, with no fanfare, Dafydd Iwan and his band walk onstage and settle behind instruments and microphones. It has fooled no one. The tent erupts into a thunder of cheering. Immediately the music begins and Dafydd Iwan's voice rises above it. "*Rwy'n cofio Llywelyn, byddinoedd Glyndŵr…*" The audience begins to sing with him as he reaches the chorus… "*Ac wrth feddwl am fy Nghymru…*" and everyone sways with the beat of the drums and guitars.

It is apparent that this is more of a cultural rite than a mere musical performance. Everyone already knows all the songs. Dancing and movement seem to be part of the whole. The band moves smoothly into its rousing version of the folk song "*Moliannwn*" and the pavilion becomes an echo chamber of clapping and singing. The tall teenager in front of me splashes beer from his glass with each chorus, and two girls bob up and down, mindless of all but the music. There is no time to take a breath. *"Mae'r Saesneg yn Esensial"* has begun and the atmosphere becomes more frenzied with each verse.

Finally, after three numbers, a break in the music. Dafydd Iwan takes a breath. The audience calms down to a dull roar. The beer stops sloshing and the dancing stops for a minute. He grins at the sea of faces looking up at him, says something loudly to them in Welsh which I don't understand until I hear him say, *"Croeso, Sandi o Galifornia"*, and the audience responds with loud cheers and clapping. He obviously said something like "Welcome, Sandy from California". I am shocked, but I don't have time to linger on it. He grins even bigger and announces (in Welsh but this time I'm ready for it) that I am in Wales to learn to speak Welsh! This is magic now. The audience roars and stamps and claps its approval while he smiles a huge smile and points at me. I feel a part of this crowd now. I feel welcomed into the world of *Cymro*. I am amazed that he did this. But I am also aware of how brilliant it is. An American here to learn Welsh. What better propaganda for the language? What better boost for their pride of self? His words were to them. After all, just half an hour ago he had stated to me, "You don't speak Welsh". But this Welsh was easy and his pointing arm and smile at me said, "Good for you!" It is a gift to me. It is a gift of pride to his people.

This man, so short, compact and soft-spoken in person, assumes the stature of a giant on stage. *Bendigedig*. The Welsh word meaning great, fantastic, blessed. He is blessed with tremendous charisma, a sense of *"hwyl"*, a rapport with his audience. They are blessed by having Dafydd Iwan, who sincerely cares about what happens to Wales, and he is blessed by the fervour and joy they show in his music. The performance continues, and the singing, dancing, sloshing and arm waving begins anew. The group of middle-aged women that I saw with the flag under their arms now begin a celebration of nationalism, the cultural rite of a Dafydd Iwan concert. They unfurl the banner, the huge *ddraig goch* billowing over their heads, and worm their way through the crowd to the front of the stage. There they dance to *"I'r Gad"*, the flag held up so that "Dafydd" can see it as he sings. It still flies over the crowd as the beginning strains of, "*Yma O Hyd*" start, and now every arm in the pavilion stabs the air exultantly to the chorus. "*Er gwaetha pawb a phopeth Ry'n ni yma o hyd*" "Despite everything we are still here."

From somewhere in this mêlée the little green-vested woman emerges and moves toward me. She smiles at me with her highly proprietary air, puts her arm around my waist and gives me a motherly hug. I smile back, barely able to hear in the thunder of patriotism taking place around me.

She looks up at me, then up at Dafydd Iwan on the stage, and shouts "Did he say 'hello' to you then?" It was her gift to me. She needs to know.

I smile and nod.

She beams, eyes delighted. "Are you enjoying yourself then?"

I can see that this is important to her. I smile again and nod. It is all she needs to hear. She gives me a little wave and vanishes out a side door. I know that I must think some more about all this, but I store it away for future pondering. Right now I am compelled to be part of this audience.

They are now loudly into "*Peintio'r Byd yn Wyrdd*" and the teenage boy in front of me raises his glass in a toast towards the stage. He holds it towards Dafydd Iwan like a salute, and it conveys infinite regard. This young audience, peppered with the middle-aged, is engrossed in the music and full of enthusiasm for it and the words being sung to them. They are a PART of the performance. No drugs, no fighting, no police – just beer, music, a good time and fervent patriotism. They've heard all the music before. He's sung it a million times. They know what's supposed to be done. He expects it from them. He flips messy sheets of words over on the music stand beside him. He swabs a blue towel across his forehead, and then wipes his forearm across his face. He glances at his wrist-watch. In one sense it is almost rote. But the energy radiates from him and he beams with enjoyment nonetheless.

It isn't until he begins "*Hen Wlad Fy Nhadau*", however, that true passion fills his voice. These young people sing now with great seriousness and intensity. Their arms stab the air, fists closed, in a silent show of love of country. They hold the pose throughout the song. Onstage, Dafydd Iwan is singing in lovely harmony with eyes closed. His ecstasy is Wales.

It is written across his face. "*O bydded i'r hen iaith barhau.*" "Oh, may the old language continue" – every arm in the pavilion stabs at each of the words. Then it is done. The concert is over. The youngest ones clap and stomp, wanting more, but the older ones turn away. They know he has finished.

We walk quietly back across the wet grass to the dark car park. It is almost one o'clock in the morning and it has been a long day. The drizzle begins again but I am lost in my thoughts and don't feel it touch my face. The entire evening has had an almost surreal feel to it. I ponder on this little country of Wales and its people: the gate steward who noticed Americans "asking for" Dafydd Iwan; the little woman in the green vest, so eager that I should meet him and so anxious to know I enjoyed the evening; the young reporter, spotting me as American instantly and wanting to talk; Dafydd Iwan himself, willing to meet a stranger and to tell the crowd about me. There had been warmth towards me from all of them. Perhaps it came from recognizing that I had warmth for them, respect for their culture and language. And, sadly, an almost amazed reaction that someone from that huge land across the sea, would be interested in their little world – which is, after all, the whole world to them. I think of an analogy, that of an unwanted and abused dog in a kennel waiting for death to approach, no one knowing or caring that within his soul is a fine, brave, noble and loving heart. But if a warm and caring hand reaches out to it, once its suspicions and fears are allayed, it responds with all the warmth of its great, needy heart. I think that has been Wales for a long time now, and the amazement that the Welsh people have value which is seen and appreciated by others, still stuns them.

I lie awake for a long time, although it is now after 2 a.m., reliving swirls of the kaleidoscope that was the concert. The raindrops softly slide down the window. The last thing I remember before drifting off is seeing once more the face of the little green-vested woman as she looked up into my eyes. There was such a light of pleasure on her face when she saw me enjoying her world – "her" concert, "her" Dafydd, "her" Wales.

"You don't speak Welsh" – Dafydd Iwan's flat statement refuses to go away.

No, I don't speak Welsh.
Not yet.
But I think I looked into the soul of Wales tonight anyway.

Dydd Sadwrn: The Problem With Wales

This morning, over the typical Welsh *gwely a brecwast* fare, I continue to ponder over the amazing evening the night before. The slight, harried woman who serves us our fried eggs, bacon, mushrooms and toast struggles with the door to the kitchen. I can hear BBC Radio Cymru and the barking of her little white Westie from the other side of the door. Her two-year-old grandson comes wheeling into the dining room on a plastic pedal car and she scoops him up and pulls him into the kitchen with her, scolding him gently in Welsh. He chatters back in "baby" Welsh. I think how strange it is to be in this house, having slept in one of the bedrooms, and now eating at their dining table while they make do with our presence for money's sake. It is strange to be an American in Wales. We have no anonymity. The Welsh seem to have an attraction to "American-ness" and I can't understand why. They are interested that we are there in their daily midst, and concerned that we should like it in Wales. Yet by a million little things, our clothes, our accent, our presence, we are seen as American instantly. We cannot pass as Welsh.

We can respect the culture, learn the language, like the people, and love the whole of it – but we are still separate from all of it. We are still strangers in their Welsh world. It is hard to break down barriers and stereotypes. I feel a strange guilt that this woman must serve me food, rent me her room, speak English to me when she is obviously *Cymro*.

As we carry our luggage down the odd, twisty stairwell with threadbare patches of carpet, I see the silent desperation of barely "making ends meet". The funny little "toilet room" with the frosted glass door, where the only light is from the bare hallway bulb outside the door. The dark, winding staircase up to the next floor where the "bathtub room" is. The neat but faded bedroom with its chipped dressing table and stool. I feel shamed by the stereotypical perception of Americans as "affluent", knowing that most Americans aren't by American standards, but here in Wales those standards are not the same. I am touched by the quiet dignity with which the woman takes our money, by her gentle smile and her wish to us to have a safe trip. I wonder what she really thinks about us.

The streets of Porthmadog have a bleak look this morning, after all of yesterday's rain. The grey sky has a drab, washed out quality to it. We decide to drive towards Bala and past Bala Lake (*Llyn Tegid)*, and the further east we go the less the grey sky imposes on us. There are even occasional bursts of sunshine that light up the green hillsides for a moment as we travel through Cwm Prysor and past the fame-haunted drowned valley of Tryweryn. *Llyn Tegid* sparkles with white-caps, and as we get out of the car for a look the wind rips at us in cold bursts.

Mae hi'n wyntog! I think to myself in Welsh. It is WINDY!

We follow the tracks of the Bala Lake Railway around the lake to the tiny village of Llanuwchllyn. The few stores are closed, but in the darkened window of one shop is a big gold disc proudly propped up so all passers-by can see it. It is a disc awarded to the local men's choir by Sain Recording Company for so many recordings sold. There are cobwebs leading from the disc to the corners behind it. Obviously it has been on display for quite some time. Obviously it has tremendous importance still in Llanuwchllyn.

On south now, down towards Aberystwyth. Every bend in the road brings a vista of misty distant mountains, emerald green hills, pale lavender, bushy bracken, sheep and stone farmhouses tucked into little *cwms*. The valley names are poetry – Cwm Dyfi, Cwm Einion, Cwm Ceulan. This is a country of breathtaking beauty.

We reach Aberystwyth in time for dinner at a hotel across from the Prom. It is a chilly night and the sea is choppy, waves running high up on the beach. Protected from the wind by the glass window of the dining room, we look out at the bay as we sip coffee and dessert wine. I think, for the umpteenth time today, about the concert in Porthmadog and meeting Dafydd Iwan. I am somehow haunted by the brick wall of his statement "You don't speak Welsh." There was a closing off of the smile on his face, a shutter on the welcome in his eyes. There had been such resignation in the flat, dead tone of the statement. It makes me feel sad. This hugely vibrant, energized public persona – this one-man "bandwagon" for all things Welsh, had seemed so serious, quiet and prone to moments of deep thought when met in person. And his comment, "You don't speak Welsh", now seems to me to be the great problem with Wales.

Dydd Un Deg Un: Seeds Of Hope

Rhys is back!! We are all so glad to see him. There is an air of relief with us to see Rhys instead of a new stranger with another new dialect, someone who may not be so careful, organized and insistent on our good pronunciation of Welsh. Our security, at this point, is frail like our confidence. Our progress in the language is measured by each word we recognize by sight and sound, and remember how to say. Each precious phrase we understand has been hard won, and the wrong *tiwtor* at this point could knock it all down like a house of straw. So, relief for all that we won't have to fear now. We know Rhys will not knock us down.

We start off with a listening game called "Mr and Mrs". We are given "mates" whom we must answer questions about. First we must listen to Rhys read the question to us in Welsh, understand it, and then respond in the appropriate Welsh. I can understand about 85%, enough to get context and meaning so that I can answer. This amazes me when I think about it. Although I often despair, I realize just as often how much I now know in Welsh! How much I now understand in reading and listening. How many words I now own.

We spend some time reviewing Friday's units – a little of this, a little of that. Would that be said *hwn a hwnna*? This and that? All I know is that in this type of language course it can almost always seem to be *gormod!* Too much to retain! Our review of letter pronunciation and vocabulary is fun because it is in the form of a game of hangman. Everyone has their own small, personal triumphs. Mine are pronouncing *w* correctly and figuring out that the word on the board must be *cwpaned* (cup), and knowing that *cŵn* is the plural of *ci* for dog. However small a piece of scrabble is, scrabble piled on scrabble builds a house.

Rhys gets off on a tangent that is a favourite of his. Modern colloquial Welsh. It is what he refers to as "baby Welsh", and he uses the example of *coffi fi* meaning "my coffee". He says it is the way two-year-olds would talk but everyone says it so it has become a part of the new

Welsh. Hmmm, "baby Welsh" seems to about fit my level of speaking so it is nice to know that some of my "baby Welsh" is appropriate. "My coffee" is not exactly a truly useful expression but, nonetheless, I know how to say it. It is *hen ddigon* for me right now – more than enough.

At the break we sit across the table from our half-day substitute *tiwtor* of last week. We sip our cappuccinos and eye her warily, but she smiles and asks how the *cwrs* is going. We look at her, wondering how to respond. All I can think is *Mae hi'n anodd!* It IS difficult, that is the truth. She can tell by our expressions, our silent evasiveness, that it has not been an easy week for us.

"Don't despair," she says. "The seeds are being planted now, and someday, to your surprise, Welsh will bloom."

We want to believe her! If only I could have had the bloom of Welsh on my tongue when I met Dafydd Iwan, instead of the stigma of "You don't speak Welsh... "

"It's the truth," she says, laughing at the wan, hopeless look of disbelief in our eyes. "I've seen it happen again and again."

We smile back at her, the seeds of hope having been planted in us, if nothing else.

Dydd Un Deg Dau: You're Speaking Welsh!

Monday morning and another full day in the *dosbarth*. Back to class. The weekend is a thing of memories now. It still vividly lives on the edge of my mind, but there are other things on our *tiwtor's* mind today. It is what Rhys loves to do so well the first thing in the morning, move us around the room with a list of questions to ask of each other. In Welsh, of course.

I struggle through the "How do you say?" bit. My vocabulary words are all there. *Dim problem!* But oh, all those verb tenses – oh, those mutations! Some people seem so brilliant, so knowledgeable, so totally prepared! Mair never makes a grammar mistake, her pronunciation is perfect. Telor knows every word, plus the local everyday uses of each word. Nigel knows every noun in the Welsh language I think. Beth, politely, in that English way she has, points out my errors by saying, "Don't you think?" or "It ends THIS way, doesn't it?" She never points the verbal finger of blame at ME, just subtly shows me the right way. I sometimes feel so dense. But in my own defense I remind myself that Mair has Welsh-speaking parents, Telor has lived in Aber all his life, Nigel has a Welsh wife and has studied this before, and Beth works in a Welsh-speaking office. None of them have come into this "cold", as I have done. Still, this morning I am feeling lost.

At the morning coffee break I see Angie sitting in the sunshine under a tree and go over to her.

"How are you with this course?" I ask. She rolls her eyes and groans. "Do you ever feel out of your depth and over your head?"

"All the time. Always!"

I look at the sky for a minute and the truth dawns on me. "I could stop the course right now and go back and repeat the first two weeks again. Then I might understand it better."

She looks at me. "I'd need more than that!"

"Why are you taking this anyway?" I ask her, suddenly curious about why she is subjecting herself to what she seems to consider torture.

"The company I work for is Welsh and they work with Welsh speakers, so they want everyone employed with them to know some Welsh." She considers for a minute and shakes her head. "They're paying for me to take this course, but at this point I'm in over my head I'm afraid."

Gwen, from Canada, is leaning against the brick wall near our tree. She has been listening to Angie and me and now comments, "You don't seem to understand any less than anyone else in class does. You seem to be right on with it."

I am surprised at this. I look at her to see if she is serious but she is already thinking ahead. "As far as I can see everyone in class feels like you do. No one feels like they understand it all. No one feels like they can speak Welsh."

I think about this. It's kind of a sinking and swimming situation. Our head goes under and then we come up for air. Occasionally we get in a few good strokes and then we are pulled under again. Is that how learning a language is? Especially when one embarks on an odyssey to learn it so fast? Two weeks ago very few of us really knew much about Welsh. Now we know many words, can pronounce them with a half-way decent pronunciation, and are even speaking in phrases. That we can understand what is said to us entirely in Welsh, and can read and translate some Welsh, is really a little miracle. Maybe we just want more, expect more, than is humanly possible so fast.

Lunch time comes and goes. We start the afternoon with a game of Bingo! All numbers must be called in Welsh, and all numbers are time numbers. Time is one of my favourite things because it is easy. I don't have to worry about verb tenses with time and the numbers are easily learned. *Pum munud wedi naw, hanner awr wedi chwech, canol nos.* Five minutes past nine, six-thirty, midnight. On it goes – the numbers of an hour or part of an hour – hypnotically droning – until Bingo! Finally!

Methodically and clearly we learn more verb tenses. I came, she came, they came. By *trên*, by *bws*, even by *hofrenydd* (helicopter). "*Des i, daeth hi, daethon nhw.*" Then clearly, methodically, we are taught necessity.

Mae rhaid i fi. I must. I must be careful. I must not speak *yn Saesneg!* Speaking in English is now the ultimate sin in class. *Mae rhaid iddi hi fod yn ofalus!* She must be careful too. And he, and you, and we. None of us can speak *yn Saesneg nawr.* It is not allowed.

At the break I walk down the hall and open a fire door. I see a strange new Welsh word. " PULL." I pronounce it unconsciously. "Peelth." I wonder what it means. The realization dawns. OH! PULL. Pull! I pull the door towards me. All right! It's English! My head is too full of Welsh words, they have crowded out the English! It is the most exciting discovery of the day. I can actually mistake English for Welsh, so immersed have I become in the new language.

Over coffee I marvel at how my own language can suddenly look strange, and how a strange language can suddenly look familiar. I wonder if that is what our substitute *tiwtor* meant yesterday, when she said Welsh would bloom to my surprise? I glance at a magazine lying on the table. There is a huge advertisement on the back that proclaims "*S'dim byd yn ddu a gwyn!*" I think – "Nothing is black and white." Easy as that: I read the Welsh and knew what I was reading.

Back in class Rhys throws vocabulary at us rapidly and we have to put each word into a sentence. Word after word becomes sentence after sentence. He picks up the pace and so do we. Excitement shines in his eyes.

"Yes!" he shouts. "You're speaking more Welsh than I thought you could! Listen to yourselves! You're speaking Welsh!"

And we are.

Dydd Un Deg Tri: The Brick Wall Of Welsh

Revision Day. This is to be said in the tones of one announcing the Apocalypse. It is Doom's Day. It is the day when I have to use all of those verbs – present, past, future. Not to mention the various "yes" and "no" words, ten at last count. I remember when I struggled with *ie* and *nage*, or even the harder *ydw* and *nac dw*. But now there is *fydd* and *na fydd*, and *gallwch* and *na allwch*, and *gwnaf* and *na wnaf.* Do I know when they are all to be used? *Nacdw!* I don't!

I must be careful to remember *(cofio!)* all those fearsome *treigliadau* too. Those monsters in the words – the mutations. I'll have to know that *beth* or *yr* or *ar* or *y* or *am* means that *p* becomes a *b*, *t* becomes *d*, *m* turns into *f*, and *g* goes away completely. I must know that many things cause *p* to be *mh*, *c* to be *ngh*, *g* to become *ng* – but what those many things are I'm still not quite sure of. Is it when there is an *yn*? Or is it a *fy*? Or, is it both?

When do I mutate? Which verb is it? What ending do I want? How do I say it? What am I trying to say anyway? Does this mutation go soft or nasal or aspirate – as I feel I will at any minute! Oh no! There are also the negatives! *Sai'n* and *so ni, does dim* or is it *s'dim*? *Pido*, or is it *peidio*, or *beidio*, or *peidwch*?

"*Ers faint dych chi'n dysgu Cymraeg?*" Translated: "How long have you been learning Welsh?" I could say, "Not long enough", or I could say, "Too long", or I might even say, "AM I learning Welsh?" But I suppose I would have to answer, "*Dw i'n dysgu Cymraeg ers dwy wythnos.*" Response: "Two weeks? "*Jiw, jiw!*" Translated: "Well I never!" Yes, today is The Day.

A day of games and contests, questions and interviews. In Welsh. *Wrth gwrs!* Of course! A day of listening to tapes and trying to understand. "*Sai'n deall!*" "I don't understand!" Or, more miraculously, "*Dw i'n deall!*" "I DO understand"! By the end of the day I know more than I did at the beginning of the day. That always seems to be the case with revision. My fear and dread turn into fun and games, my sinking feeling into confidence that I actually have retained something. Never denying that it is difficult, but stunned that things seem to have stayed with me. Today is the moment of truth, and the truth isn't as bad as I suspected.

After class I go to the Pioneer Market, buy a copy of *Y Cymro*, and I sit down to browse through it. In total amazement (and with some pride) I discover that I can gather enough contextual meaning, from the Welsh I now know, to understand the basics of the five articles I read. I don't know every word, but I am reading and understanding. I know the basics of the language now. I know quite a few words. It is only a matter of stringing it all together into coherent sentences and having the courage to attempt to speak it. To take a risk, chance – speaking in Welsh to someone. But with who? I ponder this eternal Welsh dilemma.

I think again of my meeting with Dafydd Iwan, but this time in a whole new context. He reached out, shook my hand, smiled, spoke a greeting in Welsh and I stood there – a non-Welsh-speaking rock. Smile faded. Realization dawned. "You don't speak Welsh." It wasn't a new discovery for him. It had happened many times before. The brick wall was me, not him. The recognition that this was a non-Welsh-speaker was as old, discouraging and heavy as the last time, and the time before that, when Welsh was spoken and not understood. It was a familiar, disheartening experience. The flat, dead monotone of "You don't speak Welsh" was that gamble, that risk realized. How sad it seems that the Welsh-speaker must always have to confront that question. Will they speak Welsh? And now I, too, must face the dilemma. It's scary to think of testing my fragile confidence in public. If they don't speak Welsh, well all right. They won't know if I am speaking badly or not. But what if they DO speak Welsh? Will they look at me as if I am from Mars, full of contempt for my poor Welsh? I decide to wait for another day to test the waters. I am not yet ready to proclaim publicly that "*Dw i'n siarad Cymraeg!*"

Dydd Un Deg Pedwar: The Truth About Wales

The morning is bright with *heulwen*. There is nothing so pure and clean as sunshine after a night of rain. Class begins with a *stori*. We have to piece together the story from slices of paper with Welsh sentences on them. It is a story about Tecs (American, *wrth gwrs!*) and his *reiffl* (*wrth gwrs!*) and he is robbing a *banc (wrth gwrs!)*. New verbs. *Pwyntio* (which is what Tecs does with his *reiffl*) and *sgrechio* (which is what the customer in the *banc* does when he *pwyntio* his *reiffl*). It is a typical stereotype of the average American day.

"On the spot!" exclaims Rhys to each version we concoct of this un-Welsh story.

It is a day filled with words. New words. Adjectives – the best kind of words. And how much better in Welsh!

Hyfryd: Lovely. A delicate word, as lovely as its sound.
Hapus: Happy. With a joyous lilt to it.
Trist: Sad. Melancholy in the gentle way it rolls over the tongue.
Caredig: Kind. A soft, caressing word reminiscent of love.
Twp: Stupid. Silly sounding and fun to say.
Crac: Angry. Short, sharp and hard.
Byr: Short. A brief little word like the lack of height it describes.
Ffwdanllyd: Fussy. And it is, with its silly-looking double *f* and mushy *lls*.
Blewog: Hairy. It looks and sounds like a harmless monster.
Clustdlws: Ear-ring. Literally, ear jewel. How much more glamorous to wear an "ear jewel" than a plain old ear-ring in your ear!

Then there is the endearing Cambricized Welsh word created for that modern miracle machine, the microwave. A *popty-ping!* How auditorily graphic, how verbally wonderful. *Popty-ping! Popty-ping!* It entices the tongue and insists on a repeat performance. But my favourite word of the day has to be *blodau haf,* or "summer flowers". It is the Welsh word for "freckles". *Blodau haf* – how much more bearable freckles become when thought of as summer's flowers! The beauty of the Welsh language is this sense of poetry that underlies so many of its words. It is no wonder that the Welsh call their language the "language of Heaven".

Despite this feast of words, however, people in class seem tired today. Worn out. Overloaded with words, perhaps. Crammed full. Bilious with verbs. Bloated with mutations. For the first time they wish not to return after the break. Cerys leaves, saying something is wrong with her tongue – no words will come off of it correctly today. She says her head is tired, unable to think. "There's no more room," she says. "If I stay here I'll start crying, so I'm going home."

I relate. I was there a week ago myself. I know the sense of frustration she's suffering. We all arrive there off and on. Somehow we go on. *Meddwl.* To think. *Credu.* To believe. We think too much, we believe too strongly. We think we have to learn *yr iaith*, we believe it is a necessity. It is *pwysig iawn* to us – very important indeed! And yet *annhebygol* – improbable. Maybe even *amhosibl.* Is it really impossible though? Maybe we just get discouraged too easily and too often.

We all say we know too much too soon. Therefore we feel like we know nothing. *Dim byd!* There is no time to sort it through. Some of us say, "Oh, sure we'll go home speaking Welsh. We can all say '*Ble dych chi'n byw?*' That's surely fluent." The cynics grin and feel the futility of it for a minute. The optimists in the group shake their heads at the pessimists.

Nigel looks tired. He has a cold (the communal class cold we have passed around like the boxes of Kleenex we share). He has circles under his eyes. He's suffering from reality check. He now knows, as we all now know, that it will take us years – not days or weeks or months – but YEARS to do this thing called *Cymraeg*. His Welsh-speaking wife will have to wait to discuss the world situation fluently with him. He's afraid she will be disappointed. He hopes she will speak Welsh to their expected child so it will be spared this torture.

Our break ends on these notes of despair and depression. The faces are long as we enter the classroom. We sit down at the tables glumly, looking at Rhys as if he stepped off of the moon.

Rhys looks at us and utters one word. "*Cymro.*"

We look at him expectantly and he says, "What does it mean?"

"Welshman." Everyone says it with confidence.

He shakes his head. "No."

Our eyes stare at him blankly.

"The truth about Wales is that everyone is judged by *yr iaith* – the language," he explains. "It is always a matter of 'Do you speak Welsh or don't you?' If you speak Welsh you are *Cymro* – part of the sacred brotherhood of Welsh speakers. If you don't speak Welsh you are *Sais*. English. Pejorative. Negative. It does not necessarily refer to where you live or come from, but which language you speak." He stops to look at us.

Texas-bred Jenny asks, "You mean you don't have to be Welsh to be *Cymro?*"

"A lifelong Welsh person, born and bred in Wales, can be *Sais* if all he or she speaks is *Saesneg* – English." He smiles at our confused faces. "A family where the parents spoke Welsh but didn't pass the language on to their children is despicable – and *Sais*. If – IF – you are English, or Welsh, or American, or whatever and live in Wales and speak *Cymraeg* then you are *Cymro*. Part of the accepted people. Fellows together in Welsh."

He stops again and laughs. The look on all our faces seems to delight him. The teasing look he sometimes wears flashes across his face. "AND – if you've taken and finished (survived!) an Wlpan class or two, well, then you are a notch up on the scale. Not *Cymro* – but not *Sais* either. You see, the attempt is there. You are on the way."

We all look at each other in various shades of amazement. Was this man prescient? How did he know the conversations that had taken place at the break? How did he know that this was exactly the right moment to discuss *Cymro* with us? Did he realize how he had just jerked us up out of the depths of despair into hope?

He stares back at us nodding his head. "It is a very important distinction, the ability to speak or the desire to speak carried into action, "*yr hen iaith*" – the old language. As opposed to the lack of desire to speak, or even hostility to speaking, the language."

I think ever again to the Porthmadog concert, and Dafydd Iwan announcing me to the crowd, and that I was there to learn Welsh. It suddenly takes on greater meaning and significance for me. A tiny crack in the *Cymro* door, as Rhys had explained it. *Sais*, yes, but the intent to speak Welsh was there and therefore maybe a little notch up on the judgement scale. The certainty that one is judged by *Cymro*, by what you don't speak, lay there in that ever present "You don't speak Welsh". And now another layer of meaning is unveiled for me. The complexity underlying all the seemingly trivial events that night in the *Cymro* world of the rugby field in Porthmadog stuns me. My naivety, my innocence, my foreign perceptions overwhelm me in light of the revelation laid out for us by Rhys. What an insular, fiercely loyal, fanatically bonded world *Cymro Cymraeg* is! How a part of me yearned with desperate longing to be a part of that world too. The possibility of it seems as remote as life on a distant planet, and I understand the quiet despair that Nigel must feel, with his *Cymro* wife, and he shut out of that clannish world of Welshness even though he, too, is Welsh. That the dark depths of turmoil in this little country centre on the language has become even more apparent to me. What bitterness there must be, what resentments! To be judged by not speaking the language you were robbed of learning – the perceived smugness of those fortunate enough to have had *yr hen iaith* from birth. The *Cymro* and the *Sais* – the "have's" and the "have not's" of language.

Our last new phrases for the day are ones with which each of us can relate. *Wnei di fy helpu i?* Will you help me? Or, more commonly, *Wnei di'n helpu i?* It is a plea we have all felt like making lately. Even more so the next expression – *dros ben llestri*, "going over the head". Just today we all felt that we have gone over our head, and ninety-percent of us probably have!

Rhys, omniscient as he seems to be, looks at us kindly, actually even fondly, at five o'clock and says to us, as we turn for the door, "*Paid, paid digalonni!*" "Don't get disheartened. Don't lose heart!"

Dydd Un Deg Pump: A Lovely Myth?

Last night we spent two hours at the pub with a Guinness and our homework for today. Despite the chatting, drinking and Welsh rock music the homework got done, so today I am prepared and positive. Besides, the sun is shining and the sky is a clear, cloudless blue. How can I not be positive on a day like this? I have no complaints at all!

Strange, then, that our first unit in class today is about Complaints. Anything I've ever wanted to complain about I can now do in Welsh. There are all kinds of words for complain too, can't complain about lack of choice!

Cwyno.

Achwyn.

Conan.

There is a wonderful word for the verb "to grumble" – *grwgnach.* It sounds exactly like what it means. The word itself grumbles. *GRWGNACH!*

There are lots of attitude phrases too.

Paid grwgnach! Don't grumble!

Beth sy'n bod? What's the matter?

Beth yw'r broblem? What's the problem?

And the ultimate attitude – *Beth dych chi'n disgwyl i fi'i wneud?* What do you expect me to do about it?

Can you change it? Can you fix it? Can you make it better? Can you believe this?

Na allaf! No, I can't! And I woke up positive this morning.

A miracle happens before morning *coffi* break. Rhys talks about pronunciation. The great secret is finally revealed! I learn, at last, how to make *ch!* This is what Rhys says that Welsh speakers do with their tongue. They place it back and up almost to the uvula. I try it. Marvellously, it produces the moist, phlegmy sound associated with *ch!* I try it again. It happens again. At last I know where to put my tongue! It is a huge victory on the road to pronunciation. We are all making the sound now and it sounds like a TB ward, but there are smiles of achievement everywhere. WHY didn't someone explain this to us two weeks ago? As a footnote, Rhys also brings up the *ll* sound and demonstrates how to make it by putting his tongue forward at the ridge of his mouth and blowing outward. The result is the "thl" kind of sound real Welsh speakers get with *ll*. Rhys says it is like a baby about to spit out something it doesn't like. I wonder, watching him make the sound again, how Welsh speakers manage mealtime conversations!

After the break we are run through a series of oral reviews of verbs and vocabulary together. Rhys gives us a sentence in English and we answer by translating the sentence into Welsh aloud. Everyone does one and then we do many as a group. He runs us through tenses of verbs, flinging vocabulary words here and there in each new sentence we are given.

He's fast!

We're faster!

Finally he stops, looks at us with a huge smile and says, "*DA IAWN!*"

We look back at him with tight little smiles of pride.

"The first week I had you, by the end of the week, you were talking like two-year-old Welsh babies." He pauses to look at us again. "Now you are approaching Welsh five-year-olds. My congratulations!" It is the ultimate accolade.

We laugh, but we feel good. It is an achievement for sure. How many people do I know, anyway, who have the vocabulary and speaking ability IN WELSH of a five-year-old? It is almost a miracle to go from *dim* (zero) to this in less than three weeks! After all, *rhaid cropian cyn cerdded.* One must crawl before walking.

After lunch we practice our complaints by complaining to Rhys that mae'r *cwrs 'ma yn rhy ddwys.* There are groans and nods to accompany this complaint. We all agree – the course is too intensive.

"*Paid grwgnach!* Don't grumble! It's called 'intensive Welsh', remember?" Rhys responds good-naturedly.

He has just explained sub-rule number whatever – only a "small sub-rule" according to him. How the Welsh language loves to break its own rules! We have just discovered that the apostrophe is used constantly to show that letters have been dropped. " Oh yes, by the way, just wanted to remind you that a letter is missing here and you can guess which one it is, IF you know the rule."

There's always one of these "small" sub-rules to remember and Rhys is breaking us down with them today. He knows he is.

"*Mae Cymraeg yn rhy hawdd,*" he jokes.

Yeah, sure it is – Welsh is too easy. Ha! As easy as growing tusks or turning into a wild mushroom maybe. I CAN learn it though. I tell myself this regularly with a few sub-rules: IF I am in the right frame of mind; IF I can inspire myself with the concept of the 'sacred brotherhood of *Cymro*'; IF I convince myself I can find Welsh speakers who will tolerate my learning; IF I can keep my sanity; then yes, I CAN learn Welsh.

To prove this I launch into reading the interview that Rhys passes out to all of us. It is in Welsh, *wrth gwrs*. Of course. We are to translate it into English. The interview is with a woman named Siân Lloyd. This means nothing to me. I have never heard of her before. I turn to Angie, my afternoon partner, and ask her who Siân Lloyd is. She tells me that she is a weather person on TV in Wales. I express my amazement that a weather person is a celebrity in Wales. It seems strange to me, because in America there are so many local channels on television that one single weather person just would not stand out. Every county has a TV station, and of course there are many counties in each state – and fifty states! And every station does weather! Angie smiles and patiently explains to me about Wales.

"You see, it is such a small country." She shakes her head in perplexity. "It seems that most people really do know most people in some way. Maybe not directly, but by connections with other Welsh people at least. Many Welsh people have so many, many connections that they can almost always find someone who knows someone else. Or, they know that person's brother, or sister, or mother, or father, or cousin, or son etc."

"You mean the old saying I always hear is true? Everyone in Wales knows everyone else?" I ask.

She laughs. "Well, probably not quite, but you hardly ever meet a Welsh person who doesn't know something – something directly personal

– about a famous, or semi-famous, Welsh person. They have either met them, or know someone who knows them, or are related in some oblique way, or do business with them, or lived by them once, or have a relative who does. So, the intense interest in Siân Lloyd is like any other famous person that way.

It is just too hard for me to believe. But I again recall Porthmadog and the little green-vested woman and the gate steward. They had seemed to have such proprietary ownership of Dafydd Iwan. It seems to fit with Angie's explanation. If true, if the communities are so cohesive, then can there really even be such a thing as a "star" in Welsh society? Is "celebrity" merely a matter of being known by everyone's cousins' best friend or next door neighbour? It is a concept beyond the grasp of an American, but completely endearing to contemplate. I wish to believe it and almost convince myself that it could be true, but Angie herself destroys the illusion. I tell her about the concert in Porthmadog, about meeting Dafydd Iwan.

"You met Dafydd Iwan? Oh my God! Mair, Mair – she MET Dafydd Iwan!"

Mair looks up with huge eyes. "Did you talk to him?"

I nod my head, stunned by their amazement.

"Oh WOW! I can't believe it!" Mair turns to Nigel. "Nigel! She met Dafydd Iwan!"

He eyes me with awe. "That must be the most exciting thing that has happened to you in Wales! My God! I mean, did you actually MEET him?"

Cerys has been listening to all of this and she now chimes in. "Good God, do you mean he actually stood there and talked to you? Dafydd Iwan? You're *jocan*!"

By this time I am laughing at all of them, and at myself too. There goes the endearing belief I had almost convinced myself was true. "Wait, wait – I thought that in Wales everyone knew everyone else."

Angie looks sheepishly at me. "Well, it's MOSTLY true." She starts to laugh too.

So much for the myth. But it is a lovely myth nonetheless.

Dydd Un Deg Chwech: You Will Never Forget

It is Friday, and although not the 13th, it is a bad luck day anyway for our *tiwtor*. Everyone is in class this morning but Rhys. Apparently he slipped off a curb the night before and had to go in for X-rays this morning. So we are on our own. As the good, dedicated class that we are, we sincerely review our homework aloud and discuss it as we do each morning. Then we play the two review games that Rhys had left for us. Somehow it takes us only half the time it takes us to do it with Rhys; we don't understand his directions, and everything seems to fall flat. We all feel like saying, *"So hwn yn gweithio!"* This doesn't work! We aren't good enough at Welsh to plough ahead without a teacher!

About ten fifteen Rhys hobbles in on crutches with his foot in a cast. He sees our eyes staring downward at it.

"Yes," he says. "It's broken."

We all make sympathetic sounds, and in the best tradition of teachers, he gallantly sits down, swallows two pain pills and carries on with the unit. The review game goes much better with his presence once more and we make it to the morning break after all. To our horror, Rhys hurtles himself down the three flights of stairs he has only recently struggled up on his crutches. He feels too depressed about his foot to even consider spending *amser coffi* by himself in the sterile white box of a classroom.

Break time reveals that: Gwen is homesick for Canada; Cerys is suffering from an attack of nerves over a job interview; Beth is worried about a computer foul up in the office where she works; Lowri can only think about Saturday's game at the Millennium Stadium where Wales will meet Canada; Angie is looking forward to getting home to her *cariad*; and everyone else is just relieved that it is Friday!

Rhys manages to haul himself back up the three flights of stairs with a lot of moral support from the rest of the class. He swallows two more pain killers and begins a new unit on Asking Permission.

"Ga' i dy boeni di?" May I trouble you? (to learn more Welsh on

Friday mid-day before a weekend?)

"*Na chewch!*" No, you may not!

We will mouth it, we will parrot it back to you, but Cerys has a tension headache, Lowri has to pack, Angie looks at the clock and Nigel sighs repeatedly. Rhys grimaces and cringes with each hop to the blackboard and back to his chair. Telor shows me his "new" Roman coin his coin dealer just sent to him. It has the head of Julius Caesar stamped clearly in the tarnished black silver.

"Twenty pounds! *Dau ddeg punt!*" chortles Telor triumphantly.

I handle it with awe. "Twenty pounds? And it's real?"

"It's real." He grins.

Everyone else is now staring at the coin and Telor hands it around for others to hold. Rhys sighs. He has obviously lost control. So he makes the best of the situation.

"Numbers Game! Let's guess the age of Telor's coin – in Welsh, of course." He has our attention again and on we go. *Ceiniog* is penny. *Punt* is pound. *Cant* is one hundred. BUT – remember – sub-rule – all currency is feminine so soft mutations are running loose here.

Telor loses interest and turns to me to talk. He gives me another lesson in Welshness – or the "us and them" syndrome.

"My parents are of what I call the 'chapel culture'. They are a little 'mafia' of people who are not only on every committee in town, but RUN every committee they are on. Their life is one continual meeting." He shakes his head. "Not only that, they are completely *Sais.*"

I forget the lesson Rhys gave us on *Cymro* and *Sais* for a minute. "I thought you were born in Aberystwyth."

"Oh I was. I mean *Sais* as in not speaking any Welsh. They see everything Welsh as being subversive. They think Nationalists are obsessive troublemakers." Again he shakes his head and sighs. "I made the mistake of saying *Pen-y-bont* for Bridgend last night and I thought I'd never hear the end of it!"

I am fascinated. It seems so hard to understand this mind set. I, too, shake my head.

"I mean, they REALLY came down on me! And these are native

Welsh people you understand! They make up nicknames for Welsh speakers. They call them "Nats" or "Nashes", and think they speak Welsh and call towns by their Welsh names just to stir up trouble!" He thinks for a minute and then smiles, giving a snort of laughter. "They're going to be fooled though. Welsh is getting to be so "in" to learn that someday half of the people in Wales will speak Welsh. I'll be one of them too."

He already speaks it better than most of us in the class. His whole office is Welsh-speaking, and he is determined to be the same. This is his second time through the beginner's Wlpan course and his understanding surpasses everyone else's.

"I'm a 'Nat'!" he confides in me suddenly, with a quick, mischievous grin.

"So am I!" I whisper back at him and he laughs.

It's noon and someone asks Rhys, "*Gawn ni fynd i ginio?*" Can we go to lunch?

Rhys glances at the clock. "*Gallwch.*" Yes, you may.

And we do.

It is two o'clock on a Friday afternoon and everyone is here but Rhys. He's late, but that is all right with us. We are thinking of the future this afternoon. Who is going on to the second level of Beginning Welsh, who's got to get their thesis written for their advanced degree, how we will miss each other. Jenny passes around a sheet of paper for everyone's e-mail addresses. We all worry about who our final week's *tiwtor* will be. How can anyone replace Rhys? A card is passed around for us to sign and we all contribute *pum deg ceiniog* (fifty pence) to pay for the box of chocolates we are going to give to him. We wonder where Rhys is.

It is two fifteen when he hobbles into the room, apologizing to us for his lateness. Jenny stands up and presents the card and chocolates to him while we shout our rehearsed line,

"*Diolch yn fawr, Rhys!*"

He blushes and stares at us, a big smile crossing his mouth and entering his eyes. He opens the card and silently reads what we have all written, then looks up at us.

"This makes it all worthwhile," he tells us. "I have truly enjoyed this class and teaching you Welsh." He glances down at the box of candy. "And 'chocy's'! My favourite. *Diolch!*"

Call it karma, call it irony, but our last lesson with Rhys is on "The Future". We groan at the thought of a second set of new verbs to learn in one day, but he reassures us that it is a "very positive lesson". We begin the chant of the future – *gwela i, gweli di, gwelith e/hi, gwelwn ni, gwelwch chi, gwelan nhw.*

We look at Rhys and mutter, "*Ddysgwn ni byth!*" with heartfelt sincerity. We will never learn!

"*Ddysgan nhw byth,*" says Rhys to the ceiling with a heartfelt sigh. They will never learn.

"*Beth yw'r broblem?*" he asks us.

Our problem? We will never learn all this!

He smiles. "*Anghofi di ddim.*" You'll never forget.

We want very much to believe him. Maybe it is true. But Cerys is thinking of her job interview, and Nigel of school starting, and Lowri of *Cymru* vs. Canada, and the others of Friday night beers at the pub. Rhys himself is thinking of having to tell his wife about his broken foot, and five o'clock can't come too soon.

As I walk out of the classroom my eyes see only the Welsh words on doors and wall posters in the hall. I see English, but read it as Welsh, struggling to fit it into a Welsh pronunciation until I realize that I'm reading English words. I find myself misspelling in English suddenly, putting Welsh spelling in the words subconsciously. My mind runs thick with Welsh words, Welsh sentences. I try experimental questions and answers in my head – all in Welsh. I begin to realize how Welsh has subtly begun to permeate my thinking. There is always so little time for introspection, but, on my own for awhile like this, I suspect that it may be even as Rhys said.

"*Anghofia i ddim!*" I will never forget!

Dydd Sadwrn: The World of *Cymro Cymraeg*

Today sparkles! The sunshine glints off the sea, the green hills shine, the sky is a vivid blue. And above all, it is Saturday! I have decided to make it a "touring weekend" because it is our last weekend in Wales. I will not be in class tomorrow so won't know who our new *tiwtor* is until Monday. It just seems important to have more of Wales in my memories than to be in class. So, today sparkles and we are off to *Gogledd Cymru* again. North Wales is in my blood.

Driving north from Aberystwyth, I see painted slogans calling on me to protect the Welsh language, and it reminds me of the large stone wall near Aberystwyth which has been spray-painted "*Cofia Dryweryn*" on it in bold white letters. "Remember Tryweryn" – the infamous Welsh valley flooded by the English to create a reservoir to pipe water to England. I am familiar with the Welsh history of the sixties, but driving towards North Wales is the first time I see visual proof that the bitterness still remains.

I realize that North Wales is Nationalist Wales as we approach the vicinity of Caernarfon. Several times near Pen-y-groes and Bontnewydd I see road signs written only in English. Underneath the English words are painted, in green paint, the Welsh word. In one case, the English word has been smeared out with a swath of green. The campaign for the Welsh language seems to be ongoing here in the stronghold of the Welsh Party, whose *Plaid Cymru* posters adorn many telephone poles. As we enter Caernarfon I see "*Cymru am Byth!*" scrawled across the side of a building. "Wales Forever!"

The car park beside Castell Caernarfon appears to be full, but we manage to find a spot to squeeze into. Above us *y ddraig goch*, the red dragon of Wales, flutters from the battlements of the castle. Sails on the boats in the harbour snap in the breeze. The white-washed walls of Caernarfon Castle reflect the sun and its ramparts gaze benignly down the streets of the city. They are busy streets full of Saturday shoppers. I notice that the streets are also scattered with trash and litter, but, just as I wonder why such quaintly charming streets are so badly cared for, a street sweeper turns the corner. Shoppers step out of its way as the big brushes whisk up paper and garbage.

We join the people milling in and out of the shops, wandering through Welsh jewelry and crafts stores, ever the typical American "souvenir hunters". I find what I have been searching for, a small silver dragon on a silver chain. It seems appropriate that I would find it here in Caernarfon, where the dragon flies from the English castle and "*Cymru am Byth!*" shouts from the wooden wall down the road. I fasten it around my neck, feeling the little dragon nestled into the hollow of my throat.

Past the buildings of the *Cyngor Arfon*, the Caernarfon Council, and into the business section where the regular, everyday shops are, the crowds change. No longer are there tourists everywhere, spilling over from the castle. Now there are appliance and clothing stores, chemists shops and bakeries. I hear Welsh words being spoken by the cluster of people I pass on a corner. A window display catches my eye and I turn into a little shop full of Welsh cards and music CDs. I browse through the cards, testing my Welsh as I attempt to translate the messages inside. I choose two birthday cards and then thumb through a rack of CDs. I discover a new one by the Welsh rock group *Anweledig* and add it to my purchases which I take over to the lady behind the counter. This lady has been discreetly eyeing me since I entered the store and I feel that I have "American" written all over me. Now she looks at my little pile of purchases, and as she rings up the price of the CD she again eyes me with bright curiosity.

"I've been selling a lot of these lately. You know this group then?" Her eyes stray over me and I can read "American" in them.

"Yes, I have another CD of theirs." I smile at her. "I heard them sing last week in Porthmadog."

"Ahh." She looks at me with a wondering gaze that drives me on to explanations.

"I really went to hear Dafydd Iwan, but they were also singing there." I smile lamely.

"You know of Dafydd Iwan?" Now there is intense curiosity in her voice and I know for sure that she is another little green-vested woman. I can read between the lines of her questions to the real thought behind her eyes. "But you're American."

"Yes, I own all his music."

She picks up the two birthday cards to ring up the prices, then gestures to me with them. "You must be able to read these." It is a comment but there is a subtle question mark in it.

"Yes, I can. I'm taking Welsh at the university in Aberystwyth. But reading Welsh is a lot easier than speaking it!" I smile and hand her the money for my purchases.

"*Diolch.*" She says shyly, smiling at me.

"*Diolch i chi.*" It comes out so naturally that it takes me a moment to realize I had spoken in Welsh to a Welsh person!

This is like opening the floodgates! Her face becomes sunshine and radiates it towards me in a huge grin. "*Diolch yn fawr iawn, llawer o ddiolch!*" This is followed by a tide of Welsh that I can't begin to understand, but the intent was there. I can see her change before my eyes because I spoke Welsh back to her. I smile and nod and exit the store. I feel like I have been given a birthday present, a Christmas present, or a gift that surpasses even that.

I look around, realizing that I am smiling at the whole world. My first public utterance of Welsh. Three very simple words. But they had caused such an amazing reaction, and I feel so amazingly happy about it! I walk along the street dodging shoppers, my mind elsewhere. Was it that I attempted to speak in Welsh to her, or that I could read the Welsh cards, or had told her I was taking Welsh, or that I mentioned knowing something of the popular music culture in Wales, or was it all of it combined? What had taken me from "American tourist" to "I will smile and speak Welsh to you" status? Again I am overwhelmed at the warmth and friendliness of *Cymro* when that magical barrier goes down. This validifies all of my days of struggle and frustration. This amazing language thing! I feel inspired, now, to keep at it.

It begins to drizzle. From out of nowhere, seemingly, the sparkle of the day has faded to grey clouds. Umbrellas go up as we head to the car park, and, by the time we leave Caernarfon behind, the rain has begun in earnest. Huge drops pelt the windshield and dribble down the side windows. The Roman ruins at Segontium look drab and lifeless in the sullen light as does the neglected, weedy cemetery further along the road. Past the little village of Waunfawr the road opens into what must be vistas of the mountains of Eryri on a clear day. Caernarfon and its suburbs are behind us now and the Welsh countryside reclaims us.

As we round a twist in the road we see a field of sheep with a Border Collie pursuing them over the wet grass. A man stands in the rain watching them, the rain dripping off of his tweed hat and down the shoulders of his tweed coat. Through the drizzle we can see eight or ten cars parked alongside the field. A soggy sign on the fence post says "Sheep Trials Today". Intrigued, we rashly turn in at the gate and drive down the muddy, sloshy lane towards the other cars. A group of men are standing around the back of one of the cars talking. They are dressed in varying hues of woollen jackets and caps, green rubber boots pulled up to their knees with chunks of mud and goo splashed over them, and all of them turn to stare as we pull up and park.

The rain is still coming down, making rivulets of water on the windows, and it is difficult to see out into the field where a hazy figure is whistling signals to his dog. I can just make out the black and white of the dog's coat against a bleary group of sheep. They clump together and then break into a run with the dog close on their heels. The figure whistles and both sheep and dog veer to the far corner of the field. Another whistle. The dog breaks toward the sheep and they split into two groups. A black and white flash of fur as one group dashes into the pen in the middle of the field, but the other group of sheep run off the field before the dog can reach them. The tweed-coated figure and the Border Collie walk after the sheep as the rain pelts them.

I wipe the condensation from my side window to see better and meet the eyes of six Welshmen, all still staring at us from their cluster at the back of the car next to us. There are no smiles on their faces. They don't attempt to speak to us. They just look pointedly at us as if we are aliens from a distant planet who happened to drop from the sky onto their sheep-dog trial. One of them says something to the rest of them in

Welsh and they all laugh. I feel like a voyeur who has been caught peeping through a window into the *Cymro* world.

A stocky, tweedy, booted man in a red woollen cap walks brusquely past the group of laughing Welshmen with a small dog at his heels. He stops beside our car and leans into my open window. Grey hair wisping around a weathered face, ruddy cheeks glowing, I realize suddenly that it is a woman! She speaks abruptly to her dog, who sits instantly. Her voice is loud and hearty with a distinctively British accent.

"Rather nasty weather isn't it?" she asks me.

I nod and smile.

"I thought I'd better give it a go anyway. I haven't been at this long. Every dog so far has been perfectly brilliant and I will go out there and make a muddle I'm afraid." A booming laugh and then a sharp command to her dog here. "Well, I'm off!" The dog stands. She reaches down and picks it up by the nape of its neck and tosses it over the fence. Then she climbs over the railing after it. The drizzle and mist devour them, but from what I can see she and her little dog perform "brilliantly".

We watch for about a half hour and then everything seems to come to a halt. A young man in a dark green raincoat walks up to our car and leans in.

"Just stopping for a spot of tea. We'll start again in a while." He has a friendly smile and twinkly eyes and a decidedly Welsh accent. "Are you Americans then?"

Ah ha. Here it is. The curiosity is going to spill over at last. Someone has gotten up the nerve to find out about us. I notice the clusters of Welsh-speaking men have all turned their eyes our way once more.

"Yes. From California," I say.

"Ah, California – I imagine it is dry and hot there about now isn't it?" He laughs.

"Dryer than it is here!" I also laugh and he leans his arm on the window ledge.

"Interested in sheep trials are you?"

"Well, we have a herding dog ourselves, so we like to see how other dogs go at it."

This information seems to change everything for him. The curiosity blooms into excitement. "Do you now? What kind of a dog do you have?"

"A Bearded Collie."

His eyes are dancing and his accent deepens as the words roll out. "A Bearded Collie? Why, I have one of those too! He's not here today because he's working, but he's the smartest dog I've ever had. I don't have to teach him anything more than once. He remembers everything right away! Had to go clear up to north Scotland to get him. Where did you get yours?"

"In California. They are a fairly popular breed there actually. They have a lot of herding trials and agility trials, and Beardies do quite well at both of them."

Amazement now fills his eyes. "In California? Really? I had no idea! Who would have thought it!"

The clusters of men have moved in closer to our car. I glance past him out of the window and I see that the flow of Welsh has completely stopped. Over their thermos cups of steaming tea they seem to be leaning in to catch this conversation, which is drawing to a close now as the rain begins again in full force.

"Well, have a good journey." The young man beams at us as we roll the windows up. "Ta ra!"

We back up and the cluster of Welshmen move away from the car. The young man waves at us. We wave back. Then, miracle of miracles! The clustered Welsh-speakers all smile and wave at us too! We drive down the lane in a flurry of spattering mud and they are quickly lost to our view. The gentle green hills, softened with mist, close around us and I settle back to think over the experience.

If only I knew more Welsh! This could have been a time when I could speak it and maybe made the difference. I had again been an "alien in a foreign world", and once again the initiative of a curious Welshman had bridged the gap. If only I had the courage to do the gap bridging! My hunger, my need, my thirst for Welsh has never been greater than it was right at this moment. How must the little silver Fiat, spattering mud, zipping up to the fence with its load of Americans, have seemed to the startled clusters of men peacefully standing in the rain and comfortably speaking their Welsh? Probably the same way it seemed to the green-vested gateman at the Porthmadog concert.

"You don't speak Welsh."

And if I did, the acceptance would have come a lot sooner back there in the rain-sogged parking field. Oh, this proud, prickly, curious and innately warm world of *Cymro Cymraeg*!

Dydd Sul: Glaw

I wake to the sound of birds outside the window and I stare at the high ceiling of the Judge's Chambers. Having driven to Betws-y-coed the evening before, we had found a room in what was once the old courthouse. Each guest room was named according to its function as in court days. Now the re-plastered old walls which had seen many judges' decisions saw only sleepers. From the pale yellow light at the edge of the window curtain it looks like a sunny day. It is still early. I feel in no hurry to get up.

I think back to yesterday afternoon, tucked snugly away from the rain in a little *tŷ bwyta* in Beddgelert, still pondering on the world of Welshness over carrot cake and a pot of Darjeeling. Then dinner in Betws-y-coed and the late evening walk we took across the suspension footbridge beside the shadowy churchyard. Afterwards, sitting in the cosy lounge in over-stuffed chairs by the electric fire, we read the newspaper we had brought from Caernarfon and I practiced my Welsh with *Newyddion Cyngor Arfon*'s Welsh half. Betws-y-coed is a tourist mecca, with its pretty buildings, leafy trees and stream running through the heart of it. But it does not seem Welsh to me. It seems like an extension of England, a bit of tailored nature too tainted by the hordes of people who wander its length during the daytime to be appealing. I can't say what it is about it that makes me feel this way. Certainly it IS in Wales, but I hear no Welsh being spoken and there is no sense of Welshness about the place. I ponder over what this mysterious 'sense of Welshness' is. Surely it is apparent in Aberystwyth and Caernarfon, and just as surely it is absent here in Betws-y-coed. It is an intangible quality that speaks to the heart and says, "THIS is Wales".

Later, as we eat our eggs, bacon, tomatoes, mushrooms, toast and coffee in the breakfast room, I look at the other guests and again feel that somehow I am not quite "in Wales" here. I am anxious to move on, get back into 'real' Wales again. So it is ironic that we decide to backtrack a bit and visit the city of Llandudno, for it is about as far from 'real Wales' as any town can get and still be in Wales.

It is one of those mornings that are rare and wonderful here. Clear, sunny, warm and barely a breeze anywhere. The view of the sea and cliffs from the seafront promenade goes on forever. The streets of Llandudno are painfully neat, utterly English, extremely prosperous looking. Spiffy Victorian hotels and guest houses fill block after block, and the road is lined with Jaguars, Mercedes, shiny new Volvos and BMWs. Most noticeable, however, is the absence of the Welsh language. I look and look but can't see any signs in Welsh. 'Wales' is just not here – it is a pocket of Welsh Englishness where the English language reigns supreme. On benches along the beach sit grey-haired, dumpling-shaped Britishers, speaking English without the lilt and musical cadence of a Welsh accent. The only flag I see flying is the Union Jack. Hotels have names like "The Queens Inn" and "Prince Edward Arms". Along the seafront is the modern and impressive looking North Wales Theatre – bravely flaunting its Welsh title of *Theatr Gogledd Cymru*. I think how odd it is that it should be in Llandudno, of all places! How did it not end up in Caernarfon, or some other bastion of North Wales-ness? Perhaps a shiny new theatre in North Wales relies on the people who drive the Jaguars and Mercedes and BMWs. Certainly the economically depressed people of much of North Wales do not have the resources to support such a place. But the irony of proudly calling it Theatr Gogledd Cymru in a place like Llandudno can't escape notice!

Perhaps it is this barren absence of Welshness, or perhaps it is just *hiraeth* for Welsh Wales that turns us back, in a loop, towards Caernarfon. Once more Welsh words appear and all feels right again. We cross the Menai Strait to Ynys Môn where we loop through a string of very Welsh villages with very Welsh names – Brynsiencyn, Dwyran, Aberffraw. We stop to walk through fields of sheep to Bryn Celli Ddu, a neolithic burial chamber. The huge stones form a cavern large enough for several bodies, reached through a low, narrow entrance tunnel. There is absolutely no wind. The air is calm and warm, which I think must certainly be unusual for this bleak, windswept-looking island. We have the grassy path to ourselves, except for a couple walking their Corgi and comfortably speaking Welsh to each other (and presumably the dog!). This is a new thought for me. A Welsh-fluent dog. Even that Corgi may understand more spoken Welsh than I do!

Back in the car we turn south for Aberystwyth once more. Back through Porthmadog once again, with its spectacular views of mountains and bay, and on down through Harlech with the haunting grey castle on the hill. Down through the beautiful green valleys and steep hillsides of grazing sheep, and then back into the rain and clouds. My thoughts are also rain and clouds. I have left North Wales behind and I don't want to leave it. I don't know when I will return. The thought of going "home" to America is too unbearable to dwell on, but it is inexorably approaching. I feel the first fingers of the black depression that will descend on me next weekend. I love Wales with all my heart and soul. This is where I want to be. This is where I belong.

Now I am starting to know the language. I have begun to feel at ease with the *Cymry* I meet. I am learning the land as a person who lives there does. Wales feels like it could be home. I love the long, mysterious words of towns on signposts. I can pronounce them, I know what they mean, I can understand the variations from area to area – why *f* vanishes from *dref* near Aberystwyth and becomes *dre* or why it is *tre* instead. I'm getting the mutations figured out, I can speak and think whole sentences in Welsh. I don't want to have to stop now!

I love the grey stone villages, the old chapels and ancient oak trees, the Welsh flags flying from buildings and houses and the big, proud stickers on car bumpers. I love the only graffitti I've seen – "*Cymru Rydd*" and "*Cymru Am Byth!*" sprayed on rocks. I love hearing Welsh being spoken on the streets, and I hate that I can't understand enough of it to make real sense of the advertisement I hear on the radio about "*Dafydd Iwan a'r Band*". Something about "*Medi*", and I sigh to think that in September I will be back in California.

I realize that in a sense I am romanticizing Wales. Intellectually, I know that the Welsh people don't just attend Dafydd Iwan concerts and dance around waving flags. I know that those sheep on the hillside are eating thistle and weeds as much as good grass and that the poor grazing land reflects the plight of the poor farmers. I know that unemployment is high and wages are low, that housing is scarce and too expensive, that the youth of Wales are leaving their country behind, the chapels are dying, and the struggle is incessant and eternal for the survival of the Welsh language and culture. It's just that all of this is part and parcel of this land I love. That I feel concern and anguish for the problems, hot anger over the injustices, fierce pride in the nationalism, deep affection for the language and people – that is all part of Wales, for me. I have begun a love affair with Wales that I can never end, and that I must return to America is my private sadness. *Mewn hwyliau trist iawn heno* – a sad, sad mood tonight.

Dydd Un Deg Saith: Hirwen

With both curiosity and trepidation I go to class this morning. Who is the new *tiwtor* this week? My question is answered as I enter the room. My first impression is of a grey-haired mother hen, plumply fluffed feathers and alert bright eyes. Her facial expression and physical carriage say "No nonsense!" But the smile that lights up the face is sweet and pleasant. In hushed voices everyone tells me her name is Hirwen. I can't decide if it is awe or raw terror on their faces, but I settle into a chair as she turns to the class and speaks.

It is a blitz of Welsh!

A wall of Welsh!

A hailstorm of Welsh!

A diving-off-a-high-board-into-a-deep-sea of Welsh!

We are swimming for our lives!

We are grabbing any word we recognize as a lifebuoy!

Here an *enw*, there a *mewn*. We float up onto a *gwaith cartre* and take a breath.

Our minds struggle to translate into English as we grasp another familiar Welsh word and slide it into some context of meaning. But the words haven't waited for us! Somehow they have gone on to new sentences and we leap to grab another word and another.

Gwrando! Listen!

Welsh is pouring out like a fountain of words.

Do we understand?

Uh, yes – no – maybe.

No one is smiling. The faces are sombre, intent, gazing inward as the language-mind listens. What is she saying? What are we doing? What does she want from us? Do YOU understand? I think so. Well, fifty percent at least. Make that a big PERHAPS – a big MAYBE NOT. Our eyes grab at each other across the table. *Helpwch fi!*

We must NOT write – only listen. No words will go on the board.

We will only repeat over and over and over. *Bydda i 'ma, Bydda i gartre, Fydda i ddim yn ôl, Fydda i ddim yng Nghaerfyrddin.* I long to see a word! I long to verify with my eyes the sounds I'm attempting to make! What happened to the rights of visual learners?

Bydda i'n enwog. Bydda i'n gyfoethog. No, I'll never be famous or rich. *Fydda i byth yn siarad Cymraeg!* She didn't say that but I'm busy with the thought before I can banish it (again!) from my brain! "I'll never speak Welsh!" No, I can't think like that. *Bydda i, byddi di, byddwch chi…* on it goes.

At coffee break faces are long. Mair is happy. She says that at long last we'll be speaking Welsh, responding only in Welsh to spoken Welsh, having to think in Welsh. Angie wants to quit the class, or change classes, or just throw in the towel. No one else is quite sure where they stand. It is good to hear only Welsh all of the time, we all agree on that. It is hard, but good, to be forced to always think in Welsh. We like that. But we feel lost at the same time. It is very, very fast. It is very, very nerve-shattering. We gulp our coffee down and stare at the table, shaking our heads. It is time for Round Two.

Round Two turns out to be a game with partners, which is not difficult after the morning's Round One. It is just asking questions. Well, reading, pronouncing, internalizing, translating and asking.

Fyddwch chi'n edrych ar S4C yr wythnos 'ma? (Will you be watching S4C this week?)

Fyddwch chi'n gwrando ar Radio Cymru heno? (Will you be listening to Radio Cymru tonight?)

The reading is easy. Pronouncing I have down. Translating not too hard. But answering – there is the catch. Speaking out loud is difficult and intimidating.

Lunchtime comes quickly. I make a fast trip to town to run an errand and grab a baguette at Spar. I eat it sitting in my car watching the sea. *Y môr.* It is grey and windy and the surf churns onto the sand while my mind churns *Cymraeg* over and over. I can't seem to rest from it. The words, the sentences, turn round and round, chasing each other through my mind as the waves chase each other over the sand. I am a beach, being drowned in Welsh words. Amazingly, I seem to remember everything I repeated endlessly all morning. Hirwen told us that a word must be repeated 80 times before you know it forever! 80 times! I wonder how many Welsh words I now 'own'?

Back for Round Three. *Geiriau*. Words. I love to listen to them from Hirwen's mouth. She is a native Welsh-speaker and her English is heavily Welsh accented. It lilts and sings, up and down in improbable places. Her Welsh is flawless and I can hear all of the words I've seen being spoken correctly. It is a melodious flowing of words, link upon link. I can't begin to approximate it with my clumsy, rebellious tongue! The words flow on and on to our endless repetition. *Fi sy'n, ti sy'n, ni sy'n, nhw sy'n, pwy sy'n?* Will I remember all this without writing any notes – which I am forbidden to take?

Afternoon break and the faces at the table are smiling. Angie will stay. Nigel is *hapus*. Everyone agrees that our ears are now becoming attuned. All afternoon our comprehension level has zoomed upwards. Our confidence level has risen. Our nerves have hardened. We are thinking in Welsh words suddenly. When, today, did this start to happen? Who can say? We all 'own' a few more words and phrases than we did when we woke up.

After the break we write in Welsh our English thoughts. We all agree that it is this translating our English thoughts into Welsh words that we have been lacking. It is what we need to do. We think in English, of course. We have to find the Welsh words for our English. We have to be able to reach in and pull out the right Welsh words in the right way. It is such an arduous process, but the whole pattern is obvious to us now. It is easiest to recognize written words and to recall meanings. It is harder to hear the word and recognize it before recalling it. It is hardest to respond by forming English thoughts into Welsh words, adding mutations or dropping letters, changing to the right verb endings and tenses. We recognize how difficult it is. But our minds surprise us with how much is really being retained. With time we will sort it all out. Now we are more or less sponges, parrots, semi-thinking language robots.

Hirwen says that her husband is not *Cymro*. He, too, is a learner.

He has been learning Welsh for four years now and her comment is that he is "doing pretty well at it now". Four years, and married to a Welsh speaker besides, and he is only doing "pretty well at it now"? We look at each other in discouragement. We have only begun the hard fight – but still, no one gave up today. No one quit the class, threw in the towel. One small victory at a time.

Dydd Un Deg Wyth: What It's All About

Llwyd, gwyntog, oer – late *Awst* in Aberystwyth this year. The grey, the wind, the cold dampen our spirits as we enter the *dosbarth*. A floodtide of Welsh greeting warms us at the door.

"*Bore da! Sut mae?*"

"*Da iawn!*" We stammer a response.

They are words we know and can answer, but they are very fast and very Welsh sounding. They sound REAL!

Hirwen is very, very Welsh in looks and voice, accent and expression. Her English reflects her Welsh-speaking in its patterns. "I'll be passing the papers back now." "You're tired is it?" She takes charge instantly and makes her expectations known bluntly and immediately. Right up front the Welsh are!

We again tread the water of Welsh words. But now we are attuned, we know what's coming and what will be expected of us. We review our *gwaith cartre* and it seems we all did it right.

"*Hapus?*" She nods encouragingly at us.

"*Hapus.*" We nod back at her.

Today we will go into the future. Perfect. It's on all our minds. We learn *a' i, ei di, eith e/hi* – I'll go, you'll go, he'll go, she'll go – and we will. Only four more days now until I go from here. But, I'm here now and Welsh is all around me!

At *amser coffi* Telor comments, "Didn't she say her husband had been learning Welsh for four years and now is pretty good at it?"

We all nod our heads.

"And that's being married to a Welsh speaker!"

We all nod our mutual sense of dismay.

He throws his arms up and says, "I'd better quit now!"

We all bemoan our common fate, agree to the truth of Telor's comment. But none of us means it. That's the amazing thing. We all intend to just keep going, despite the obvious and apparent obstacles and difficulties. It is more than just stubborn tenacity. It is the neophyte climber, standing at the base of Mt. Everest and vowing that someday he'll stand on top. It is determination, inspiration, and obssession. For all of us it seems to be a compelling need. This mysterious need to learn Welsh.

Back in our Welsh world once more we must interview our partners about their choice of places to travel to, things they'd like to see there. My partner and I are given the country of *Awstralia*. It is a challenge to our Welsh vocabulary to find words that we know that fit ANYTHING about Australia. Poisonous snakes? We haven't learned it. Kangaroos? Don't know it. Koala bears? Ah ha! We do know the word for "bear". *Arth*. On we go.

We are scolded, all of us, for thinking as speakers of *Saesneg*.

"English doesn't follow the same sentence construction patterns as Welsh," she explains. "Your sentences aren't being kept SIMPLE enough. You are making it too hard for yourselves. Think in Welsh ways."

We try. We struggle to think of adjectives following, not preceding, our nouns – of something being WITH us, BY us, UPON us. We keep slipping into old *Saesneg* ways.

We like Hirwen. We like the constant flow of the Welsh words. We like that we are being forced to listen. We are amazed that we can understand part of all she says. We are stunned when she stops the class and says abruptly:

"Has anyone ever spoken only in Welsh with you before this week?"

We have been doing a translation. Half of us seem to have understood her verbal instructions. The other half seem to be doing something else entirely. Angie has admitted that she is "clueless".

"No," we say. "No one has spoken ONLY Welsh to us in the past three weeks. They have always translated for us after they have spoken to us in Welsh."

This admission brings with it realization. We have been spoiled, made dependent, been cheated of a learning process so fundamental to learning a language. Hirwen is the only one to speak completely in Welsh to us. She shakes her head in disbelief. She mentally criticizes her fellow tutors for their "weakness". With her true Welsh sense of standards and high expectations she chastises the language programme for allowing this to happen.

"You must hear Welsh! You must be forced to think in it! Every crutch must go! You have only three days left now. *Duw a ŵyr!* You have been cheated!" Again she shakes her head.

We are now feeling very deprived ourselves. We are angry at the thoughtless way we have been allowed to muddle safely around *yn Saesneg*. Her disgust rubs off on us. We look at each other with a question mark in our eyes. Where would we be now if we'd had Hirwen all along? Would we have been really speaking Welsh by now? Well, it can't be helped.

We can translate, question, read, listen, pretty much understand what we see and hear. We could not do any of this a month ago. We can't speak Welsh very well. But, we can speak it. And *Duw a ŵyr* – we all know that *trwy dwll bychan y gwelir goleuni*. Light is seen through a small hole.

Like a mother hen, puffed up with pride, Hirwen passes out papers that have the words to Wales' national anthem on it. "*Mae Hen Wlad Fy Nhadau.*" "Land Of My Fathers." I feel a thrill of excitement. I know these words! I worked hard to memorize them in Welsh. I can sing this song in Welsh. I DID sing it in Welsh a few weeks ago in Porthmadog. Now I'll get to do it again in class. I feel like I did when I was five years-old and learned the words to "The Star Spangled Banner" in kindergarten. I look up at Hirwen and I'm touched by the look on her face. It glows with excitement, pride, tenderness, and a sort of fragile vulnerability. This is important to her, this song, this moment of teaching it to her students. It means so much – *iawn, iawn.* This is everything right here. This is what it is all about and what it is all for.

She asks us to sing with her. We do. The look on her face is transfixed with love and pride. The notes swell upward.

"*Gwlad, gwlad, pleidiol wyf i'm gwlad*" – My land, my land, I am pledged to my land. Oh yes, this means so much.

I think of Dafydd Iwan in Porthmadog, his voice soaring in harmony over the crowd of suddenly serious teenagers. The look of utter love and dedication on his face at that moment is now the look I see mirrored on Hirwen's face, in her eyes.

"*Tra môr yn fur, i'r bur hoff bau, O bydded i'r hen iaith barhau.*" – While the sea is a wall to the true loved land, Oh, may the old language endure.

The old language. "*Yr hen iaith.*" We are all together here, in our love for this "true loved land", struggling to preserve the old language so that it can endure. THIS is what *dysgu Cymraeg*, learning Welsh, is REALLY all about.

Dydd Un Deg Naw: All In a Name

This morning *mae hi'n bwrw'n drwm*! The wind is blowing sheets of rain against the windows and water is bouncing in pellets off the pavement below. I sigh and grab my umbrella. Holding it at a slant, I pray that the wind won't blow it inside out as I hurry down the hill to class. My umbrella joins seven others which are lined up on the floor pooling water onto the linoleum. Outside, the rain sounds like a waterfall against the glass of the windows. Inside, Hirwen is smiling at us warmly and ready to begin.

We are going to look at "*Mae Hen Wlad Fy Nhadau*" again. Not to sing it this time, but to act out with a Welsh script the parts of Evan James and James James, the writers of the song. They were woollen factory workers, father and son – *tad a mab*. Hirwen is intent on our knowing both the words to the song and the song's history.

"Everyone in Wales knows both," she says. Then she pauses, sighs, and amends her statement. "Well, at least all *Cymry Cymraeg* do. How many of you can say the same for your country?" Her eyes focus on me. "How about in America?"

"Well, I know that Francis Scott Keyes wrote the words to the 'Star Spangled Banner', but I have no idea who wrote the tune to it. I certainly know the words to it, but I also know that most American young people don't have a clue about the words. We seldom, if ever, sing it. Sad, but true."

Hirwen shrugs and nods. "I have to admit that many Welsh rugby players don't seem to know the words to *Hen Wlad Fy Nhadau* either. They mouth the words, but don't know them. Although they are better than they used to be about it."

We learn new words to go with the concept of love for country: *annwyl* – dear, *calon* – heart, *teyrngar* – loyal. Also some interesting words that I've seen and heard but not known before: *rhywbryd* – sometimes, *rhywbeth* – something, *rhywle* – somewhere. But my favourite word today

– my personal word to claim as "owned" now – is *diddorol*. I heard it when I woke up this morning on Radio Cymru. *Diddorol*. Hirwen has used it all morning. *Diddorol*. I love the way it sounds and looks. *Diddorol*. Interesting. An interesting word to pronounce and spell. It flavours a sentence, peppers it with "interesting". *Diddorol*. Class, today, was *diddorol* for me.

I have a personal puzzle solved for me today – *'mlaen*. I've heard it in songs. I've seen it written. I've never found it in any dictionary. Now I know why. It is really *ymlaen*, meaning 'onwards', but it has been contracted and the "y" has gone missing, as they say here. Hence the apostrophe for the missing letter. I continue to grapple with the mutations. I can never truly say, "Oh, now I understand!" Every time I think I do, I meet a new mutation rule, but each new understanding opens a door to the ongoing mystery of Welsh for me.

Then there is the conflicting use of two words that mean the same thing. Hirwen is adamant that some words just SOUND nicer than other words with the same meaning. For example *brysur* and *bishi*, both meaning busy.

"*Brysur* is a NICER word than *bishi*. It just sounds nicer. But it is your choice of what to use." She makes a grimacing face as she says this, which shows us how she feels about people who say *bishi*.

She seems to have the same feelings about the words *moyn* and *eisiau*, which both mean "to want".

"These are the same words for 'wanting' something, but I wish you would use *eisiau*. It is so much nicer a word. It has a pleasanter sound than *moyn* don't you think?" She smiles encouragement at us, nodding her head up and down.

We take her cue and nod in return. I have to agree. I'm partial to *eisiau* myself. Although at this minute, looking at the clock and seeing that it is noon, either *moyn* or *eisiau* will do. I WANT lunch!

Lunchtime is *brysur*, a rush of errands in the hectic noontime traffic of Aberystwyth. The sidewalks are a crush of umbrellas as busy people hurry in and out of the shops. First to the jewelry store to pick up a silver Celtic ring I have been eyeing for weeks. Then to the little Welsh shop for a book and CD. Finally to the bank to start a Welsh checking account. I grab a tomato and cheese baguette at a bakery, gobble it on the way back to the car park, and arrive back in class at two o'clock, just as Hirwen walks in the door.

The afternoon starts with her looking at us, her class, with fond and twinkly eyes. She makes a circuit of the room, smiling at us, looking us over, her blunt gaze focusing on each of us individually. Then she returns to the front of the room and leans towards us, hands spread out on the table in front of her.

"I was told by your previous tutors that you were a very cosmopolitan class and it's very true. I find all of you so interesting *(diddorol)*." She sweeps us with proprietary eyes. "I am fascinated especially by all of the different American accents. I fear they are rubbing off on me. Last night I found myself counting the stairs, as I climbed, in Welsh with an American accent!" She demonstrates for us. "*Un, dau, tri…*"

We Americans look at each other. Her counting sounds Welsh to us. How can she think her Welsh sounds American? It is a very bizarre concept for us.

"I noticed this morning, when I had all three of my Americans up front reading parts, how differently each of you spoke from the other in Welsh. And how differently, also, you sound from each other in English. This just fascinates me, that you could all have different American accents." She smiles at we three Americans with a puzzled shake of her head.

I continue to mull over the thought that when I speak Welsh I sound American. I don't just sound like an amateur with bad pronunciation. No, I have an American-accented bad pronunciation. Worse yet. A California-American bad Welsh accent! A despairing thought blooms. If ever I learn to speak Welsh I will still be obviously an American. There is no escaping your accent.

The lesson this afternoon is about being born and brought up someplace. *Ble cawsoch chi eich geni?* Where were you born? *Ble gath eich mam chi ei geni?* Where was your mother born? *Pryd gath e ei eni?* When was he born? We repeat the Welsh words and phrases endlessly, it seems, and then we must interview each other. This becomes a very complicated process of family names and places. Hirwen drifts around looking and listening, and commenting about our conversations. She stops to listen as I reel off my family birth history.

"I find it so interesting *(diddorol)* that your parents were born in Missouri and Texas, and you were born in Oklahoma, but raised in Colorado and California! Why so many places? Don't Americans ever stay put? Here in Wales you'll find people who have lived in the same village all of their lives." She gives me a genuinely puzzled look.

I have noticed that most of the Welsh students in class have parents who were born and raised in the same town, and they, themselves, were born there or nearby, and STILL don't live that far away. They seem to stay put in this country, to a great extent. Suddenly the irony of Hirwen finding our American accents so different from each other hits me. A Welsh dialect can differ from another in a matter of ten miles! "Here we say *brysur* but in *Caerfyrddin* they say *bishi*. Here we say *moyn*, but in Caernarfon they say *eisiau*." Wales would fit into a third of the state of California, if that. And California is only one fiftieth of the country of America. No wonder we have so many accents!

Hirwen is still scrutinizing my personal family history. She glances at my paper and then does a doubletake. She has seen my maiden name.

"Thomas!" she exclaims. "A good old Welsh name that is! A good, strong Welsh name! One of the original old Welsh names! You're Welsh then!"

This isn't a question. It is a statement of fact. I can see by the blaze of excitement in her smile that I have soared in her estimation instantly with my "old Welsh name". She is beaming at me with total interest and approval. Her eyes are saying, "You're Welsh! And you're learning Welsh!" It is a revelation to me. It's all in the name! A Welsh name – it seems to mean everything to the Welsh.

It's time for afternoon coffee break, and the class sits together and chats. We're bonded, as only a group of people can be who have spent four arduous weeks learning Welsh together. Others in the room notice, and comment that we seem to be using so many Welsh words when we talk. We realize it is true. We toss them around now, joking with them, savouring the words and our ability to casually toss them off our tongues. We understood ninety percent of what Hirwen spoke to us after lunch. We are proud of ourselves, amazed and pleased. We think in Welsh sometimes now, and we love it!

Back in class again Hirwen asks us who plans to continue on in the language. The Welsh students all do, of course. The English only if their jobs require it. The Americans say if only a way were possible for them to. Hirwen tells us that courses are available all over Wales through the university and night courses, learners' societies and Wlpan. She gives us websites for Welsh learning on-line. It won't be the same, we all agree on that. Still, it is a way to keep from becoming *rhydlyd* – rusty. Although becoming 'rusty' is not my biggest concern at the moment.

Right now my concern is my deep reluctance to have to leave Wales at all. I not only don't want to have to stop speaking Welsh, I don't want to have to stop hearing Welsh being spoken all around me all day long. I don't want to stop meeting and getting to know Welsh people. I don't want to separate myself from this land I've grown to love so much. MY land – where my "good, strong Welsh name" came from. It breaks my heart to think of having to leave. I feel the sadness creeping up on me.

Dydd Dau Deg: The Crack in the Door

I arise this morning under a black cloud. Tomorrow is my last day of Welsh. I am already anticipating the void of depression that will swallow me whole when I leave Wales. I love this *Cymru fach*, this little Wales, with all my heart and soul. I am charmed, infatuated, connected, bonded by some inexplicable but deep cord to this land. I am a part of it, and it of me, in a way impossible to explain. It is a mystery of my psyche that I don't want solved. I only want to be able to stay here and that is impossible to do.

I sigh. Today is Revision Day and I have a feeling that it will be a rough one if Hirwen has her say about it. Her high Welsh standards and expectations will guarantee it. She will be determined to do it justice and get everything reviewed before any of us leave tomorrow. I will leave at noon, Lowri at two, Nigel and Cerys at three. This, then, is my last full day before the parting of the ways commence. Today we will suffer and struggle until our heads hurt, and be stretched beyond our capacity to learn!

Hirwen greets us at the door. Grey hair firmly in place, a lacey blouse with the two buttons over her hips undone so that the blouse can hang looser around her ample width, she stands straight-backed into all of her 5'2". Sweet-faced, proud, humorous, and adamantly determined that we will hear and speak only Welsh, and nothing but Welsh, all day today, she passes out sheets of paper to each of us as we enter. We stare blankly at them as we sit down.

"These sheets are what I call 'sticky situation' sheets," she announces. "These are for you to learn and keep handy. Today, instead of staring blankly at me like panic-stricken sheep when confronted by Welsh that you don't understand, you will use these as your lifeline."

I look again at the sheets of paper in front of me. They are full of handy phrases like, *Dw i ddim yn deall!* (I don't understand!), *Sai'n gwybod!* (I don't know!), *Wi ar goll!* (I'm lost!), ... *ond wi'n cael short 'ta beth*

(… but I'm having fun anyway).

As the morning progresses we come to rely heavily on these lifeline sheets. The favourites seem to be, *Yn araf iawn, os gwelwch chi'n dda* (Very slowly, please), *Eto, os gwelwch chi'n dda* (Again, please), and *Beth yw yn Gymraeg?* (What's ____ in Welsh?) Most of us can certainly relate to *Wi'n ymdopi!* (I'm coping!) and "*Rhaid i mi ymarfer!*" (I need to practice!). A little late for practice at this stage of the game, however. It is Revision Day after all.

Incredibly difficult Welsh words start to fly from Hirwen's mouth. We are over our heads immediately. We struggle to repeat them, pronounce them, remember them. Words, now, that seem too hard to ever use.

"*Diswyddo,*" Hirwen shouts. "To make redundant."

I ponder this and the light bulb goes on. "Oh, to 'downsize'!"

The class erupts into peals of laughter. Hirwen laughs until tears come to her eyes. I am completely puzzled and catch the eye of the other Americans in class. They shrug their confusion.

"That's what it means," I insist. "To downsize."

More laughter. Hirwen wipes at her eyes. The Welsh and English students go off into gales of laughter again.

"I can see it now," Hirwen giggles. "You cut everyone off at the knees!"

This is obviously a case of American English versus British English, and it entertains everyone but the Americans. We look with amazement at the giggling over a most common expression in American business, smiling at the gleeful child that Hirwen has suddenly become.

The lesson this morning is *Newyddion* – the news. It is full of words and phrases that Americans are sadly familiar with. *Lladd* – to kill. *Lleidr* – thief. "A bomb exploded", "A woman was murdered", "The children were arrested", "A window was broken", "A thief was caught". Even in Welsh the phrases sound dismal. *Gath bom ei danio, Gath menyw ei lladd, Gath plant eu harestio.* Unfortunately, these are the things news is made of, so these are also the Welsh words we must know. The depressing "news phrases" elicits a facetious response from Katie, one of the Americans.

"Cool," she utters in an overheard aside.

Hirwen begins to laugh and laugh. "Cool! That's so American! I love that word! I saw T-shirts at the Eisteddfod with the new Welsh word *Cŵl* on them. Actually, they said *Cŵl Cymru!* I just LOVE it!"

The Americans again share glances. "Cool" a 'new' word? Only in Wales.

"The Welsh invent new words all the time," Hirwen continues. "But some of them are so AWFUL! Like *sosejys* for 'sausages', or *stopio* for 'stop', or *garaj* for 'garage' when we have a perfectly GOOD word in Welsh for garage already – *modurdy* (literally 'motor house'). I can't see the point of inventing Welsh words when we have perfectly nice Welsh words for things already."

"Like *amser coffi* for coffee break?" Nigel asks, looking at the clock as everyone laughs.

At the break we all comment once more on how much more we are understanding of Welsh when we hear it spoken. Maybe fifty percent of everything she says now sinks in. It's like this fourth week our brain is finally able to internalize, assimilate, emulate, and respond. How supremely frustrating it is that just as this process has set in, finally launching us into the language, the course is ending.

After the break, we plunge into revision. We review in many ways the verbs *bydda i, a' i,* and *cafodd.* We do translations, listen to tapes, question our partners, write, speak aloud, answer in Welsh. Always we are prodded, scolded, teased, encouraged and pushed by Hirwen. Always in Welsh, *wrth gwrs.* Of course.

Revision continues after lunch with a game of "directons". Working in three's we must get and give directions in Welsh using a map that we are given of an anonymous Welsh town. I am struggling to give directions to Angie as Hirwen passes our table.

"*Mynd heibio'r capel, y banc a'r ganolfan hamdden* – uh – uh – *un* 'block'." I look up at Hirwen, who is now chuckling. "*Beth yw 'block' yn Gymraeg?*"

She stands there shaking her head, laughing and repeating "*Un* block."

I am confused. I used my 'lifeline phrase' and yet she is still chuckling at me. She can see that I am puzzled.

"'Block' isn't a word we use in Welsh. We don't think in terms of 'blocks' here. But I know what you are trying to say and 'block' will work I suppose." She chuckles again, tickled by this American expression so foreign to her Welsh way of thinking. Such an everyday common word in America to cause such mirth in this little woman!

She is staring at the necklace around my throat. I am wearing the little silver dragon that I bought in Caernarfon. As she realizes what it is her eyes light with delight.

"*Y ddraig goch o Gymru!*" She beams at me, nodding her approval. She reaches out and delicately touches it. "*Pert! Pert!*"

Yes, I wear my 'red dragon of Wales' often. It is my talisman promising me that I will return. That she finds it 'pretty' only says a part of what she really means. This is the woman who felt such vulnerable pride in teaching us her country's national song. This little dragon represents everything that she loves and believes in about her land – her *gwlad*. Her eyes meet mine for a minute, and I see an open door to her heart. We smile.

By five o'clock we are saturated, over-loaded, satiated with speaking Welsh. The thought of *Saesneg* is both refreshing and repulsive. I feel reluctant to give up the flow of Welsh conversation that we have struggled limpingly through the past hour, yet I am very ready to speak fluently again in my own language. What an undertaking to learn Welsh! How stiff and unnatural we sound as we ask our unnatural questions! Always reaching for new and unfamiliar nouns, verbs, adjectives. Trying hopelessly to string them together with the ever-changing pronouns. The *ei*'s, and *eu*'s, *î*'s and *tî*'s, *o*'s and *o'n*'s and *nî*'s and *nhw*'s, *i'r*'s and *i'n*'s and *mae'r*'s and *sy'n*'s.

Telor shakes his head in frustration. Four weeks and all he can do is ask where you plan to go this weekend and what you plan to do, where do you live, where were you born, where were your parents raised, what's your name, what do you want, what do you like, what do you need, what time is it, how much is this, a man was killed, a bomb exploded, the children were arrested. The more he thinks about it, the more he realizes that he knows. LOTS more actually! *Cŵl! Cŵl iawn!* But still, his wife is a Welsh speaker and she's going to be so disappointed that he's not coming home ready to talk about the state of the world, the birth of their son, their plans for the future, or even the health of '*yr hen iaith*' – the condition of well-being of the Welsh language – in Welsh. But he's living proof of the health of the language! As am I. As is Mair, and Nigel and Angie and Lowri and all the rest of us in this classroom. As is Rhys, and Judy and Hirwen and all the other *tiwtors* in the Wlpan programme. We are a string of beads with the common thread of Welsh joining us together. We are infected by need, addicted, obsessed, enchanted and lured by the crack in the door – by the smile on the face of *Cymry Cymraeg* when we speak a word of Welsh to them.

Bob nos and *bob dydd* – every night and every day – these classes are an ongoing heartbeat all over Wales. The beauty of it, the commitment to it – how unique in the world! The struggle to keep the language alive and viable runs like fire through the veins of those who realize it is a matter of life or death to the Welsh culture. The hunger to learn it is being nurtured and encouraged, and is spreading outside the realm of Wales itself to touch many corners of the world. Australia, France, Finland, America and Canada are all represented within our cosmopolitan Wlpan class. We are all committed to the love for Wales that burns in our souls. How can any language that does this to those exposed to it be anything BUT alive?

Dydd Dau Ddeg Un: Mae'r Gymraeg yn Fyw

I said most of my goodbyes to Wales last night. We had dinner in Bow Street one more time and the fact that we had to wait forty-five minutes in the pub for a table didn't matter. We sat and watched the local people come and go as we sipped our pints of Guinness, and when dinner finally came it was worth the wait. The drive back to Aber, through the green hills of sheep, and the sunset on the sea, were fitting closures.

As I sat writing at my desk in my little cubicle, I listened to Welsh music on Radio Cymru. Nostalgic music to me in my pensive mood. Sadness. Tears. Wanting and not wanting. Wanting to stay. Not wanting to go. Like a prisoner being dragged away to confinement, the great tide of circumstance is dragging me away from Wales. *Amser yn mynd* – time goes. How much time will have to go before I can return again? And *siŵr o fod* I will return!

This morning Hirwen has a tightly planned schedule because she knows I am having to leave at noon. We can see by the determination shading her face that everything that must be done will be done. One last time we review our *gwaith cartre*. No more homework to do now. We play another directions game with partners to review our Welsh from yesterday. Everyone takes pictures of everyone as we work. Everyone smiles and laughs a lot, and everyone's eyes look sad. Everyone says how hard it is to believe that four weeks have gone by so fast. Katie says it feels like the last day of summer camp – a little *trist*.

We fill out our personal assessments of the Wlpan programme, being truthful that we had huge regrets not to have had Hirwen, or someone like her, who made us speak only Welsh, listen to only Welsh, think only in Welsh. We can't help but have liked her enormously, this fiercely proud Welshwoman who's heart was a hundred and ten percent into teaching us her dear language.

At our last coffee break we all sign a card for her, each struggling to find something we can say properly in Welsh to her. We chat one last time, mostly about our future plans. The future is almost here now. The morning is evaporating before our eyes and it is already time to return to class.

There is one last unit left to do. Preferences. What we like, what we don't. This is fun for all of us because we know each other so well by now. Everyone is now very interested in everyone else. "*Hoff bethau.*" Favourite things. And conversely *Dw i'n casáu* … I hate… This is somehow a satisfying subject today. *Dw i'n casáu gadael Cymru.* I hate to leave Wales.

It is my turn to answer what my favourite food is. The answer is easy – mashed potatoes. But how to say that in Welsh? I know the word for potatoes – *tatws*. But 'mashed'? I take a deep breath and plunge in.

"*Fy hoff fwyd yw tatws mashed,*" I say, somewhat hesitantly. Everyone laughs.

Hirwen laughs gleefully and jumps to the board to write the tremendously descriptive Welsh word *tatws stwns*. It sounds like 'stomped' to me. Stomped potatoes? I guess that is exactly what mashed potatoes look like. We all laugh at the expression with the true affection and humour shared only by a bonded group of people. It is poignant. A fleeting moment. Time is almost done here. Hirwen looks at us and there is sadness in her smile.

"You all have the foundation now. Don't let it go. After a few weeks the freshness of what happened here will fade. What you retain is up to you and what you do with it. You mustn't drop it now. You must keep it! You have the basic knowledge to speak Welsh now. It's really just a matter of adding and extending your vocabulary. The structure has been given to you. Learn how to expand your simple sentences into conversational sentences. Work at it! Firm it! TAKE MORE WELSH!" The passion in her voice fills the room.

She doesn't have to convince me. I have spent a month seeing what the magic of learning *Cymraeg* does in Wales. How much it infuses into you as a person. The sense of real joy at understanding what I read and hear in Welsh. Of experiencing the mysterious learning process that gets into the blood, into the head and heart, into the soul itself. So it is really like something being amputated from me to leave Welsh behind. To return to America where I will be the 'lonely only' who knows anything about Welsh.

With a true sense of egalitarianism and fair play Hirwen distributes workbooks and tapes to all of us. There is a shortage of tapes and she wants to make sure that we going overseas get ours. Those in Wales can always get theirs later more easily. She makes sure the class is agreed with this decision, asking their permission before going ahead.

It is twelve thirty. I feel like Cinderella at the ball. My coach is turning into a pumpkin before my eyes. It is time to go. Mair stands up and reads our 'group composition' to Hirwen in Welsh, then presents her our card filled with our struggling Welsh messages. Hirwen's face flushes. She holds her hands to her cheeks. Her face breaks into a beaming smile and she clasps the card. Opening it, and seeing it full of handwritten messages, she just looks at us and smiles.

"*Diolch yn fawr,*" she says simply.

I must go. Everyone wishes me a safe journey. Lowri re-emphasizes that when I return to Wales I have a place to stay at her farm in Pen-y-bont. Angie reiterates this, saying to visit her in Aberangell. Nigel and Telor wish me well. Cerys says look her up in Caerfyrddin. Hirwen wishes me "*Pob lwc!*" and "*Pob hwyl!*" and says "*Gwela i chi y flwyddyn nesa*" See you next year – I wish.

I'm out the door and down the stairs before I can think or feel. To the room, drag the luggage to the car, and a whirlwind tour through Aberystwyth to snap pictures of the favourite spots. The view of the sea from the National Library – the *Llyfrgell Genedlaethol Cymru,* the promenade and the pier, the Tandoori restaurant where we ate, the shoppers rushing along the quaint streets – "*brysur, brysur*" – the little shop of Welsh things, the view of the college on the hill from the stone bridge. Then we are on our way.

We stop to eat lunch at a roadside turnout overlooking a *cwm* – a little valley whose slopes rise steeply towards the sky. Sheep graze complacently and clouds make deep shadows across the grass. It is a tide of sunlight and shadow, ebbing and flowing with the wind's movement. First a burst of sunlight, then a swift blanket of shadow racing over the hillsides, blotting out the sun. I sit gazing out the window, delaying the blotting out of MY sun as long as possible. But we must go on. The plane to California tomorrow morning will not wait.

The farther east we drive the more we begin to lose Wales. It happens so suddenly. No more *tafarns*, just inns. No more *Gwely a Brecwast* signs, just 'B&B's. No *canol y dref*, just town centres. No *canolfan hamdden*, just leisure centres. No *stryd*'s, no *heol*'s, no *ffordd*'s, just streets and roads. Just British accents. We lose *Cymraeg* before we have a chance to say goodbye.

But it's here. Right here in my own mind, on my own tongue. I have it. And I won't let it go. I have it and I will continue to learn it. I will go back to Wales. I will speak Welsh. It's here. Right here in my heart. Right now.

Mae'r Gymraeg yn fyw.
Welsh lives.

To learn more about Wales and the Welsh language…

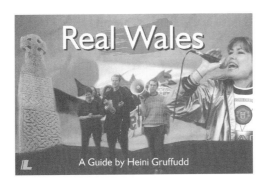

£3.95
086243 423 8

£2.95
086243 447 5

also by Y Lolfa:

The definitive dictionary for Welsh learners

£6.95
086243 363 0

For a full list of our publications both in English and in Welsh,
ask for your free copy of our new, full-colour, 40-page catalogue.
Alternatively, just surf into our website at:

www.ylolfa.com

TALYBONT CEREDIGION CYMRU/WALES SY24 5AP
ffôn 0044 (0) 832 304 *ffacs* 832 782 *isdn* 832 813
e-bost ylolfa@ylolfa.com *y we* www.ylolfa.com